The Language of the Moon
- for Beginners

Dreams, Dream Journeys, Visions,
Omens, Pictures, Myths and more

Contact: www.HarryEilenstein.de
Harry.Eilenstein@web.de
Harry Eilenstein at youtube

Production and publishing house: BoD – Books on Demand, Norderstedt

ISBN: 9783754311080

Table of Contents

I The House of Consciousness

I 1. The structure of the house

The house of consciousness is very simple and functional:

- In it there is an office with a desk on which all the data needed for the momentary situation are gathered – the waking consciousness.
This is the normal state.

- On the office desk there is a lamp, the spotlight of which is sometimes turned on and directed to a single thing on the desk when it is existentially important – the ecstasy state.
This state occurs when the subject is in fear, pain or lust, or when he is meditating in one-pointedness.

- In the house there is also an archive in which all present perceptions and all memories are present in a well-ordered way – the subconsciousness.
This archive is seen in dreams and on dream journeys. You can also call it the "dream-consciousness".

- The house itself is empty at first, but carries and contains everything else like a white canvas the picture on it or the silence the sounds in it – the deep sleep consciousness.
This consciousness is perceived in silent meditation.

- This house does not stand alone in the forest, but in a city together with the houses of all the other people. These houses are all telepathically and tele-kinetically connected with each other, creating a large network, which also has a memory for everything that has ever happened in this network. This is, so to speak, the city archive – the collective subconscious.
This is the realm of the archetypes, of the deities.

- Then there is the landscape, in which this city is situated – the fundamen-tal all-encompassing consciousness, that has no contents, but wherein every-thing happens.
This consciousness is usually called "God".

I 2. Images

These five types of consciousness differ in the amount of information that is present in them simultaneously. To each of these forms of consciousness also belongs a certain frequency in the EEG – these frequencies form octaves to each other, i.e. they are respectively twice as high or half as high as the frequency of the neighboring state of consciousness.

Forms of consciousness and contents of consciousness		
Consciousness form	Number of contents	Frequency
deep sleep consciousness	none	∅ 3Hz
„collectiv deep sleep consciousness" (God)	none	∅ 3Hz (?)
individual subconscious	all (of one human)	∅ 6Hz
collective subconscious	all (of mankind)	∅ 6Hz (?)
waking consciousness	some	∅ 12Hz
ecstasy state	a single one	∅ 24Hz

I 3. Thinking

The different number of consciousness contents in these forms of consciousness leads to different structures in these forms of consciousness, thus to different forms of "thinking":

- In deep sleep consciousness there are no contents, which means that there is also no contemplation of structures, thus no thinking.

In this consciousness one is simply there – one is just conscious of being conscious.

- In the state of ecstasy, the entire consciousness is focused on a single thing, which is why there can be no "normal thinking" here either.

In this state of consciousness, one is completely one-pointed – as in orgasm, panic or deep meditation.

- In the waking consciousness there are the contents that are needed for the momentary situation. The task of the waking consciousness is to recognize the optimal behavior in the current situation. So the thinking compares possibilities and makes a decision, i.e. it chooses one possibility and rejects the others. Here everything is evaluated and a ranking is created.

In this consciousness one is focused on one's own egoism and on the situation and tries to combine both in the best possible way – one tries to assert oneself or to use the situation in the best possible way. This "normal thinking" is therefore a selection tool.

- In the individual subconscious all contents are present. So there is no evaluation and selection, amplification and suppression, but everything is considered in the same way – the subconscious is therefore the place where one can get an overview of the whole. This means that in the subconscious things look as they are, because in a good archive everything is well ordered, easy to find and in no way distorted or distorted. Of course, this also means that the images in this archive also contain all the feelings that may still be associated with these images. So this archive is not quiet and boring and dusty, but in it it is quite alive and loud and moving.

Consequently, thinking in the subconscious mind is just the clear view of all things inside oneself – as they are.

- The same is true for the collective subconscious as for the individual subconscious, only that in the collective archive the images of all mankind are gathered in an orderly way.

The sections of this huge archive are the main themes, the archetypes, the deities and their myths. The deities also present their theme as it is. Therefore, one can learn from the deities what the wholesome form of a theme looks and feels like.

Thus, thinking occurs only in the waking consciousness as well as in the individual subconsciousness and in the collective subconsciousness. Since thinking has very different tasks in these two forms of consciousness, it also has a very different approach in both: in waking consciousness thinking is a combining of selected facts for a special pupose – in subconsciousness thinking is the ordering of all facts (perceptions and memories) in a large picture that contains a lot of different themes.

The waking consciousness depends on a good supply of information from the archive. The waking consciousness can also only make beneficial decisions if it allows the perception of all relevant information from the archive. Therefore a good cooperation between the office of the waking consciousness and the archive of the subconsciousness is essential for a prospering of one's own life.

Which means that the waking consciousness should learn as thoroughly as possible the language of the subconsciousness …

I 4. Feeling

Since thinking is clearly different in the different areas of consciousness, it is natural to take a closer look at feeling in these areas.

For the sake of simplicity, thoughts can be generally understood as "structures", feeling as "impulses" and images as more or less strongly processed "perceptual memories". The image is therefore the "vessel" that stands in certain contexts (thinking) and carries an impulse in itself (feelings).

- In deep sleep consciousness, which is without contents, the only impulse should be the "being there" – one is what one is.

The feelings are here consequently a completely self-evident "being as one is". One rests in oneself.

- In subconscious all contents are equally. However, they can contain different old feelings, which come from the time when a certain picture was created or was completed by another picture with the same theme.

If a memory is "intact", the feelings in this image are relaxed and one feels with this picture, if one perceives it from the waking consciousness, either simply a smirk or nothing at all. In the case of memories that have not yet been processed, however, the feelings in this image can urge the person concerned more or less massively to react immediately in situations that have a similarity to the image in question – either out of pleasure or out of fear.

A special form of the "emotionally charged image" is the trauma, in which the feeling of an existential threat is stored and which can therefore massively influence conscious decision-making.

In the subconscious are all the feelings that exist in the person concerned.

- In waking consciousness are the relevant contents for the current situation and are processed there.

Consequently, in the waking consciousness are present the feelings that are relevant to the momentary situation – ideally all feelings, but none of them so dominant (trauma) that the waking consciousness can no longer realistically assess the situation.

- In the ecstatic state there is only one content of consciousness.

Obviously it is just so important that all attention and consequently all actual feelings refer to this one content. Consequently, the feelings reach their

10

maximum intensity.

- Probably the same is valid for the collective subconscious as for the individual subconscious.
In it, too, all feelings are stored and are visible and effective.

Also with regard to the feelings, the subconscious archive is the place where everything can be seen as it is.

- - -

In astrology "feeling" is represented by Venus, Mars and Neptune "thinking" by Mercury, Jupiter and Uranus and "images" (or "states") by the Moon, the Sun, Saturn and Pluto.

Feelings, Thoughts and Images in Astrology			
area	*feelings*	*thoughts*	*images*
	impulses	*structures*	*states*
inside	Venus	Mercury	Moon
processed inside	Mars	Jupiter	Sun
outside	Neptun	Uranus	Saturn
fundamental			Pluto

11

I 5. The nature of the images

The images one sees differ according to the source from which they come. First of all, externally perceived images are something different from internally perceived images such as in dreams. But the inward images are by no means uniform, but can originate from quite different inner realms and then look distinctly different in each case.

I 5. a) External perception

The outer perception happens with the eyes. One sees things that emit light or that are illuminated by light when this light reaches the eye. The optical impression in the brain represents the external form of what is seen.

In waking consciousness, one perceives the entire situation; in the state of ecstasy, one perceives only the one important thing – the hungry lion, the beautiful woman and so on.

I 5. b) The transition to inner perception

The transition to inner perception is e.g. the beginning of a dream journey in which one steps through an imagined door or inwardly addresses a deity. The beginning of a daydream is also such a transition – even if not a conscious one. The awakening in the morning from a dream is also one of these transitions (but in the other direction than the beginning of a daydrem).

Likewise, the beginning of imaginations during a ritual is such a transition, or the laying of hands on a tree when one wants to converse with it. Looking into a crystal ball or a mirror is also one of these transitions, as is shifting one's consciousness into the body of another person when one wants to see what is wrong with him or when one wants to heal him. Furthermore, the conscious practice of telepathy and telekinesis as well as hypnosis also belong to these transitions. The transition from the waking consciousness to the subconsciousness shows a great variety …

From the point of view of perception as well as from the point of view of imagination, first impressions, lines, symbols, color impressions, silhouettes, etc. arise during this transition, which then gradually become clearer.

I 5. c) Perception in the Psyche

The perception or imagination in the subconsciousness (dream consciousness) consists of only slightly colored black, grey and white images. The scenery is filled everywhere with a diffuse light that has no discernible light source. Things move, the scenes sometimes change abruptly, you yourself are part of the action.

This area corresponds to the perception that is artificially evoked by hashish, among other things – however, this state is also much more easily (and moreover legally) attainable by a dream journey.

I 5. d) The transition to the Soul

At this transition, things partly start to glow from within, they become mostly colored, they have unnaturally sharp contours and they constantly change into new forms, whereby these transformations look as if clay is being deformed more and more – they are flowing transformations.

This kind of perception is typical for LSD and for quite deep meditations – it is often depicted in psychedelic art (and in the MCU-film "Dr. Strange"). Also anesthetic injections (e.g. at the dentist) can sometimes have this effect – it then looks something like the things you look at for a while seem to form bubbles and start to "bubble".

I 5. e) Perception in the Soul Realm

The images are usually still images (they do not move or change). Now and then they are symbols. They are colored and they glow from within. These pictures have a great intensity and a deep meaning that can be felt, even if it is not necessarily understood right away. Especially the eys of souls, if they appear in the inner vision in the shape of a human, are very intense.

I 5. f) The transition to the Deity Realm

Things begin to glow more intense and they also begin to become transparent. This means that you can see everything from any place. Intense feelings can occur here

13

because the boundaries begin to dissolve – which sometimes manifests itself in the vision of a bottomless abyss into which one is supposed to jump.

I 5. g) Perception in the Deity Realm

Here contours are found in the light. This realm is a continuum, i.e., there are no demarcations. Here one can only define oneself by one's own quality, but not by a delimitation – one is part of an endless continuum. This is the realm of the deities.

I 5. h) The transition to Unity

At this transition there are two important experiences:

One is home, a connectedness with everything, a rediscovery of one's own "family." The drug "ecstasy" is an attempt to bring man into contact with this realm in a chemical way.

The other experience is the "light storm", which is an completely unrestricted self-expression.

I 5. i) Perception in the Unity Realm

The perception of this realm is glistening white light or shining blackness – which is a difference only in words. This area is the unity, undivided, boundless … and fulfilling …

The "home", the "storm of light" and the "oneness" can be experienced, among other things, in dream journeys to the sage.

I 6. Why pictures?

The reason for the subconscious mind to consist mainly of images is quite simple: Language is (from the whole evolutionary point of view) a rather new invention of mankind. The sensory perception and thus also the memories of humans do not consist mainly of words, but to 80% of optical perceptions. The human being is an "eye-being".

Consequently, man still has in his subconscious the old "optical processing system of experiences" (image associations), which is also found in all other mammals, birds, reptiles and amphibians.

II   The properties of images

To understand the language of images, it is helpful to look at them more closely. The most important questions to ask are:

- What are their words?
- What is their grammar?
- What is their substance?

And as a complement to this, the question:

- Where does this language appear in a chart?

II 1.   The words of the picture language

The "words" of the picture language are the individual pictures. They are perceptions or stored perceptions, i.e. memories. To these memories also belong the impulse and the motivation, i.e. the feeling, which is possibly still bound to this picture.

Since all contents are present in the subconscious mind completely and without exceptions, there are images that come to the fore because they are more central (e.g., the image of one's mother) or are still emotionally charged (e.g., the longing for a person or the memory of an accident), but all images are in their place in this great archive.

All these images can therefore be seen in the dream – if there is an occasion that highlights these images in the night in question. This is what makes the examination of one's dreams so revealing …

In the subconscious there are no deceptions and no hiding, embellishing or catastrophising – one sees things there as they are. Each image is the best possible expression of the relevant content of the psyche – it is a memory, a reflection of a past event.

This sincerity of the images in the subconscious makes it so valuable to learn the language of dreams.

II 2.   The grammar of the picture language

The images do not stand alone in the subconscious – the language of dreams also has a grammar. This grammar is very simple: similar things make contact – like looks for like.

By this process of "thematic sorting" symbols are created – this ancient Greek word means "to bring together, to compare". This process of associating similar images with each other enables quick orientation.

This process is also the basis of "instinctive learning": similar situations are recognized again, which is the reason for either behaving like the previous time (if that was successful) or trying something else (if that was unsuccessful).

Also the training of animals (and sometimes also humans) with the help of punishment and reward uses this association principle ("Pavlov's reflex").

Finally also little children (and to some extend also adults) learn easiest by the imitation of a role model.

This association logic gives rise to a pictorial language that uses similarity rather than causality as a link.

The oldest known languages like the ancient Egyptian and the Sumerian have still partly this pictorial logic and possess hardly such logical particles like "if", "then", "but", "like", "after", "possibly", "nevertheless" and the like. Therefore, in these languages there are sentences like "Pharaoh in the palace, sun in the sky." It is not too difficult to see what is meant by this: "The mighty Pharaoh shines in his palace like the all-ruling sun in the sky." So there is a grammar possible that does not use (or use very little) the logic of causality and the logical particles …

This self-organization of the inner pictures by the assemblage of memories with the same subject leads also to the emergence of archetypes via the formation of symbols. The connection between these archetypes then finally develops into one's own inner mythology.

This mythology formation process runs in the following graphic from left to right – the effect of this mythology on the behavior of the human being runs from right to left. Of course, many more memories are combined to one symbol than only two as in the graphic – and also much more symbols to one archetype etc. The graphic is only to show the principle, how the archive of the subconscious is built up.

The Inner Myth-Formation						
outside	→ *myth formation* →				*inside*	*core*
	← *myth-based action* ←					
perception	memory	symbol				
perception	memory		archetype			
perception	memory	symbol				
perception	memory			myth		
perception	memory	symbol				
perception	memory		archetype			
perception	memory	symbol				
perception	memory				inner mythology	soul
perception	memory	symbol				
perception	memory		archetype			
perception	memory	symbol				
perception	memory			myth		
perception	memory	symbol				
perception	memory		archetype			
perception	memory	symbol				
perception	memory					

In the subconscious mind there seem to be two fundamentally different phases of activity:

- the use of inner images for orientation in the world during the waking state during the day, and

- the sorting of the experiences of the day during the dream state at night.

This "inner tidying up" is also the reason for sleep, which is actually a life-threatening affair, since during sleep one cannot perceive what is happening all around one. Thus the existence of sleep must have an existential function that just cannot be ommited.

The sleep is an invention of the amphibians, from which then the reptiles developed, which were again the ancestors of the mammals, to which also we humans belong. The amphibians invented the memory, which makes it possible to react not only with the help of fixed reflexes, but also with the help of recognition of a situation to former situations and thus learning. This is the reason why amphibians, reptiles, and mammals need sleep: to bring order into their memories and thus be able to start well-oriented into the next day.

While awake, one plays the violin of one's psyche, so to speak, which gets out of tune – while dreaming, one tunes it again.

This tidying up of the psyche creates the effect of feeling refreshed in the morning. Also the well known problem solving method "sleep on it" is based on the cleaning up process during dreaming.

Besides dreams and the grammar of ancient languages, also dream journeys, omens, visions, fairy tales, myths, a great part of poetry and many more are based on this association logic of the subconsciousness.

This principle of association is also found in some areas of physics such as relativity and quantum physics.

II 3.   The Substance of Picture Language

One can also ask the question, what do these inner images in the subconscious consist of? Are they stored materially? Are they only in the consciousness? And then there is also the old concept of vital force, which is closely connected with consciousness.

First of all, it is safe to say that memory and thus inner images have to do with the brain as well as with consciousness – a more precise differentiation in connection with the consideration of inner imagery is not necessary for the time being.

The life force can be conceived and defined in two fundamentally different ways:

   - as a "non-physical substance" which can be directed by consciousness, and

   - as a form of consciousness that can act on matter.

Taking both definitions together, it becomes clear that the life force appears at the transition from consciousness to matter. Consequently, the simplest and most practical definition of the life force is:

   - the appearance of matter at the direct perception by the consciousness without the help of the physical senses.

Possibly this sounds a little abstract for the time being, but if one has experienced e.g. telepathy or telekinesis, this form of "direct perception" becomes more vivid. Intuition is also a form of this "direct perception".

One could define the life force also simply as the transition line between consiousness and matter – assuming, that ecerything has a matter-side and also a consciousness-side.

In the description of inner processes the term "life force" is extremely helpful and also in the description of magical phenomena, where the direct perception by the consciousness (telepathy) and the direct influence by the consciousness (telekinesis) play an important role.

On the basis of the previous considerations one can say that the self-organization of the life force is based on the assemblage of similar things, thus on the association. In this way also the power animal attaches itself to a human being: The character of one's power animal corresponds most exactly to the character of one's soul and its intention for its present incarnation. The same is true for the power plant and the power stone. They represent the dynamics (animal), the attitude (plant) and the structure (stone) of the soul and its intention.

II 4.   The general structure of the picture language

When looking at the life force, it becomes apparent that it organizes itself in two more general ways besides the thematic arrangement (association) in the individual psyche: as a collective subconscious and as "vajra".

II 4. a)   The collective subconsciousness

The life force is not only found in a single human being, but in all human beings, animals, plants, minerals, etc., that is, everywhere. Since it tends to organize itself by associations, it also connects individuals with each other. This appears then in the individual as telepathy and telekinesis and in general as the collective subconsciousness. This collective subconsciousness is the life force body of humanity, which, like the individual subconsciousbess, consists of the well-ordered memories of humanity.

Therefore, in the collective subconscious there are also "central symbols", which are usually called "deities", as well as the connections between these deities, which are the "general, collective mythology".

Since the memory of the collective subconsciousness extends over the whole of mankind, the images in it also have a very long history. Therefore, when interpreting images, it is sometimes necessary to consider the history of a symbol such as the Mother, the Snake, the Barrow, the Sun, etc., not only in the psyche of an individual, but also in the collective subconscious, i.e., in the entire history of this symbol

II 4. b)   The Vajra structure

The life force of a person forms an egg-shaped sphere around him, the outer edge of which is sometimes called "aura".

This life force forms organs: the chakras.

The life force is also not static, but has an inner dynamic, which corresponds to the blood circulation in the physical body and like this is a convection current (cycle): it rises up inside the body like the jet of a fountain ("Kundalini"), unfolds at the top like a fountain, flows down again all around the body like drops, collects again at the bottom in the lake and then rises up again inside the body.

The seven main chakras have an inner dynamic: the heart chakra radiates downward through the solar plexus, the hara and the root chakra, and upward through the throat

21

chakra, the third eye and the crown chakra.

From its basic structure, the system of life force organs, that is, the system of chakras, has a simple structure:

- one central chakra,

- three pairs of chakras around this center (heart chakra), which form two rows, and

- one ray going up from the center and one ray going down from the zentrum.

The same is found in the structure of a sun:

- the sun in the center,

- three layers around the sun ("solar wind"; "shock front" and "bow-wave"), which means that a straight line passing through the centre of the sun passes through these three areas on both sides of the sun, as well as
- the two "jets" (electromagnetic fields), which lead from the two poles of the sun upwards and downwards through the three areas.

This structure is also found in the symbol of the Vajra:

- the sphere in the center

- three symbols in both directions (lotus, elephant's head, elephant's trunk), as well as

- two rays leading from the central sphere in opposite directions.

This system has many more details, which can be found in the chakra system as well as around a sun. However, for understanding the imagery, the seven main chakras are most important, as well as the fact that there are structures in the world that are found in both life force (chakra system) and matter (sun).

A detailed description may be found in my book "The Chakra System with the Minor Chakras" or in "Kundalini for Beginners".

II 5. The Moon in astrology

In astrology, the language of the waking consciousness, consisting mainly of words, and the subconsciousness language, consisting mainly of images, are embodied by two different planets: the word language by Mercury and the image language by the Moon.

So the language of images is also the "Language of the Moon".

III Associative Structures and Analogies

There is a multitude of structures that are formed in the realm of images and thus also in the realm of the life force. For the conscious handling of these images, i.e. for a translation of these images of the subconscious into the language of the waking conscious (words and causal logic), a rough knowledge of these structures is quite helpful.

There are two forms of structures in the field of images: the association and the analogy.

> - In association, two or more things with the same theme are assembled and form a multi-layered complex – e.g. all experiences with one's own mother.

> - In analogy, things with the same structure are in resonance with each other – e.g., the birth of a human being, the germination of a plant, and the sunrise.

III 1. Amorphous structures

Some of these structures have no particular form, i.e. no analogies, symmetries, poles of opposition, cycles or the like. In these structures, things have no particular geometrical arrangement.

III 1. a) Symbol

The simplest example of such a structure is the symbol, which arises from the grouping of memories with the same theme.

III 1. b) Time

A second simple example is the pictorial representation of time.

Most people live in the northern hemisphere of the earth in Europe, Asia, North Africa, and North and Central America. Therefore most people see that the sun moves from left to right along the sky (in the southern hemisphere this is the other way around). This means that in pictures the past is on the left, the present is in the middle and the future is on the right.

III 1. c)   The "slice of tree" structure

Another, quite simple structure can be found in dream journeys.

A dream journey begins by turning from the office of the waking consciousness to the door to the archive of the subconscious and then going into this archive. There one then searches for what one wants to find.

If one imagines the development of the individual subconsciousness, the picture of a tree slice arises: In the middle is the soul that has incarnated, on the very outside (bark) is the waking consciousness in the present, and in between are the annual rings that have formed in each case from what has already been there and from the new experiences. Of course, the psyche has no annual rings, but the structure in layers, which are formed by the sequende of the important experiences, can definitely be found.

This structure leads to the fact that the first thing one sees on a dream journey is the youngest layer – the outermost tree-slice ring. Then one goes back layer by layer deeper into the past. Finally, one finds what one has been looking for.

This dynamic is most pronounced when one undertakes a dream journey to one's own center, that is, to one's own soul.

This principle is also known from psychological therapy and from homeopathy. In psychological therapy, first the youngest, newest layer of a topic becomes conscious, then the second youngest, and so on, until one finally arrives at the origin of the topic. In homeopathic therapy, first the current symptom is cured, whereupon a new symptom appears which one had some years ago, which is then cured next – so symptom by symptom the healing goes back into the past until finally one arrives at the real cause of all these diseases and one is able to cure this at last.

III 2.   Circuits

A widespread structure is cycles. They are found as the daily cycle, the yearly cycle, the life cycle, the grain cycle, and the cardinal directions. They are often used in mandalas.

Almost all cycles are divided into four parts. Therefore they can be represented as analogies to each other. In the following overview some more themes have been added:

Cycles							
Day	*Sun*	*World*	*Directions*	*Elements*	*Year*	*Life*	*Grain*
morning	dawn	beyond gate	east	air	spring	birth	germination
noon	day	this life	south	fire	summer	life	growing
evening	dusk	beyond gate	west	water	autumn	dying	harvest
night	night	beyond	north	earth	winter	death	storage

III 3.   Polarization structures

Another group of structures consists of polarizations, which can have different causes.

III 3. a)   Complementary opposites

Some of these polarizations are complementary opposites, which have a whole, unhurt, neutral character. These types of opposites are in most cases (but not always) the two poles of a cycle:

- Yin and Yang	=> ever-changing life
- this world and the next	=> circle of life
- man and woman	=> creating life
- birth and death	=> circle of life
- day and night	=> day circle
- morning and evening	=> daily circle
- summer and winter	=> annual cycle
- germination and harvest	=> vegetation cycle
- active and passive	=> pulsation
- solve et coagula (solve and bind)	=> creation
- + and –	=> pulsation
- the astrological opposition	=> pulsation
etc.	

There are other astrological aspects besides the opposition, but they play a role for the understanding of images only very rarely.

The complementary opposition "man and woman" is a complex subject, which has more facets than only this simple opposition. However, for most picture considerations this simple polarity is sufficient.

The Yin/Yang principle is further differentiated in the Chinese world view by forming the combinations Yin-Yin, Yin-Yang, Yang-Yin and Yang-Yang from the simple Yin and the simple Yang. This process is repeated again, which then creates eight three-level differentiations. By combining these eight symbols with themselves, the 64 hexa-grams of the "I Ching" oracle are then formed. Here the principle of polarity and the possibility of increasing differentiation is especially important.

The oldest meaning of Yang ist "life, this side, south side of a burial mound, warm, light" – the oldest meaning of Yin is therefore „death, beyond, north side of a burial mound, cold, dark".

The polarity in the "I Ching"				
origin	*1. opposition*	*1ˢᵗlevel*	*2ⁿᵈ level*	*3ʳᵈ level*
1 Tao	2 principles (Yin and Yang)	4 symbols	8 trigrams	64 hexagrams

III 3. b) Extreme Polarizations

Other oppositions are polarized distortions of a whole state that has been lost:

- ideal and shadow
- addict and ascetic
- perpetrator and victim
- star and fan
- rich and poor
- hyperactivity and depression
  etc.

III 4. The "3" principle

A rather thick book could easily be written about the "3" principle. The tripartite structure considered here is not Hegel's "thesis, antithesis and synthesis" nor Steiner's "threefold structure", but the principle "starting point – development – end point".

Apart from the fact that this structure in itself appears in many places, there are also some more sophisticated systems based on this symbolism of the "3".

III 4. a) The Vajra

The three stages of the vajra, which can be found in the chakra system and in the structure of the surrounding space of a sun, among others, have already been roughly sketched.

In them, the basic system of "center – unfoldment – space" has been differentiated one level further, in which the "unfoldment" has again been divided into three levels.

Vajra									

surroun-	elephant	elephant	lotus	sphere	lotus	elephant	elephant	surround-
ding space	trunk	head				head	trunk	ding space

The Vajra Structure				
Area	*Quality*	*Chakras*	*Sun*	*Vajra*
center	center	heart chakra	Sun (emits photons and ions)	sphere
1st phase	impetus	throat chakra solar plexus	solar wind (area where photons and ions fly unhindered)	lotus
2nd phase	structure	third eye hara	shock front (area where the ions collide with the stardust in the surrounding space)	elephant head
3rd phase	contact	crown chakra root chakra	bow wave (wave before the shock front in stardust)	elephant trunk
surrounding space	surrounding space	surrounding space (aura)	surrounding space (Stardust in the surrounding space)	surrounding space

III 4. b) The Tree of Life

The Kabbalistic Tree of Life is the structure in which this "three-step" is most differentiated. Each of the three steps of development, which are found in the systems just described, is here again differentiated into three sub-steps:

The derivation of the tree of life			
Development	*1ˢᵗ differentiation*	*2ⁿᵈ differentiation*	*usual representation*
origin	origin	origin	
development	development-Phase 1	development-Phase 1.1	
		development-Phase 1.2	
		development-Phase 1.3	
	development-Phase 2	development-Phase 2.1	
		development-Phase 2.2	
		development-Phase 2.3	
	development-Phase 3	development-Phase 3.1	
		development-Phase 3.2	
		development-Phase 3.3	
final state	final state	final state	

For the understanding of the pictures the tree of life is only very rarely necessary – more important is the principle of the "three-step" from which it has been derived.

III 4. c) The Ba-Gua

The Ba-Gua from Chinese Feng-Shui is a simple differentiation of the Three-Step into nine areas. They are arranged in a square and represent the qualities of an area. In the representation, at the bottom edge is the entrance or similar to this area. This area can be a plot of land, a house, a garden, a temple complex, a single room, a picture, etc.

The qualities of Ba-Gua have been derived from the Tao in the center and the eight trigrams of the I Ching around the Tao.

Ba-Gua		
Trigramm: wind Ba Gua: wealth	Trigramm: fire Ba Gua: glory	Trigramm: earth Ba Gua: love
Trigramm: thunder Ba Gua: family	Origin: Tao Ba Gua: health	Trigramm: lake Ba Gua: children
Trigramm: mountain Ba Gua: knowledge	Trigramm: water Ba Gua: profession	Trigramm: heaven Ba Gua: friends

III 4. d)   The Vastu Purusha

In India, the same structure exists under the name "Vastu Purusha", which means "Nature of the Primordial Man". Since in this diagram the nine fields are each further differentiated into a sub-Ba-Gua of nine fields, a structure of 81 fields is created.

III 4. e)   The nine places of a picture

The structure of the Ba-Gua and the Purusha can be derived in a simple way that makes the character of the nine fields easy to grasp.

One can divide each area into three strips and three columns, which have a single meaning, from which the meaning of the nine fields is derived:

The derivation of the meaning of the nine fields							
Lines		*Strips*			*Fields*		
high energy		past	present	future	help	glory	ideal
medium energy					origon	topic	creation
low energy					knowledge	profession	rest

On the lower left is little energy in the past: a starting point, work, striving, learning, knowledge, practicing.

Left center is a medium energy level: one's origin, family of origin.

At the top left is a lot of energy in the past coming into the present: a helper.

In the center below is little energy in the present: the foundation, the profession, the possession, diligence, work.

In the field in the center is the essence of the whole, the theme: the soul, the self-expression, the intention.

In the center at the top is much energy in the present: the crowning achievement, one's reputation in the public eye, one's influence on the world.

On the lower right is little energy in the future: rest, relaxation, resignation, end.

On the right side in the middle is medium energy in the future: one's own children, one's own family, creative activity.

In the upper right there is a lot of energy in the future: the ideal, the goal, the dream, love, relationships.

Ba-Gua			
	Past	*Present*	*Future*
High energy	Trigramm: wind Ba Gua: wealth State: high energy in the past Quality: help from outside	Trigramm: fire Ba Gua: glory State: high energy in the present Quality: glory, crown, ideals	Trigramm: earth Ba Gua: love State: high energy in the future Quality: relationsships, happiness, aims
Medium energy	Trigramm: thunder Ba Gua: family State: medium energy in the past Quality: family of origin, heritage of parents	Origin: Tao Ba Gua: health State: medium energy in the present Quality: oneself, tempel, altar, essence, selfcentred	Trigramm: lake Ba Gua: children State: medium energy in the future Quality: one's own family, heritage to one's children
Low energy	Trigramm: mountain Ba Gua: knowledge State: low energy in the past Quality: school, learning, skills	Trigramm: water Ba Gua: profession State: low energy in the present Quality: profession, work, foundation	Trigramm: heaven Ba Gua: friends State: low energy in the future Quality: rest, sleep, sauna, pension

The application of this scheme will be illustrated by examples in the second half of this book.

IV   Images in Man

There are a lot of different types of images in man: permanent, impermanent, external, self-created, hidden, helpful, pathogenic, etc.

IV 1.   Permanent images

By "permanent images" we mean images that do not change or change very slowly. Among these images are one's own soul, one's power animal, pne's power plant and one's power stone, and in a more abstract way also one's own horoscope. Also one's own protection deity, thus the deity, of whose "sea" one's own soul is a "drop", belongs to these constant pictures.

Sometimes also two companions appear with the soul, who seem to be its siblings – if the image of the soul has one gender, these two companions have the other gender. They appear usually to a person who is in great need.

A not so constant motif is the image of one's own body, which very often appears as a house. Here the basement is the abdomen with the root chakra, the first floor is the abdomen with the hara and solar plexus, the living room is the chest with the heart chakra, the upper floor is the head with the throat chakra and the third eye, and the attic is the crown chakra. The staircase in this house is the sushumna, that is, the "life force channel" where the kundalini rises.

IV 2.   Mutable images

The mutable images consist of the memories of one's own experiences – accordingly they are constantly evolving.

These images can also be classified according to their depth, age and generality:

- general people-pictures (archetypes)
- folk-pictures (regional archetypes)
- clan-pictures (clan-fate)
- family-pictures (family-tradition)
- one's own general images (soul, power animal etc.)
- one's own changeable images (dreams)
- one's own momentary images (perceptions)

The general images in this list, such as the primordial images of the mother, birth, death, child, sex, sun, etc., are quite constant, even if they gradually evolve.

The personal images, on the other hand, are supplemented and evolved by each experience. The easiest way to get to know these images is to keep a dream diary.

IV 3.   Self-created images

There are also images that can be created within oneself. These include the use of symbols in meditation, dream journeys, magic, hypnosis, rituals and worship.

These symbols are often traditional symbols, meaning they are already present in the collective subconscious. Other symbols, such as the sigils in sigil magic, are newly created.

By using these self-selected images, one actively adds them to one's subconsciousness ("archive").

IV 4.   The discovery of hidden images

There are also hidden images or at least images unknown to the waking conscious-ness. These images and image structures can be discovered by one's own dreams, by dream journeys, by family constellations and by visions.

A special form of the hidden image is the trauma. This is the memory of an existentially threatening experience, in which the feelings of the time of origin of this trauma are still trapped, because they could never be relieved by screaming, crying, trembling and the like. The trauma images are still filled to the brim with adrenaline, so to speak. Therefore, dealing with them is difficult and sometimes they are hard to recognize.

IV 5.   The development of images

The individual images in the subconsciousness evolve through one's own experien-ces – the general images in the collective subconscious evolve through the events and innovations in human history. Therefore it is sometimes necessary to look a little more closely at the development of the general images, i.e. the archetypes, in order to understand an individual motive which is connected with this archetype.

IV 6.   Being in contradiction with the images

Sometimes you yourself are in contradiction with the images you carry in your sub-conscious mind – this can become a serious problem, because then the office of the waking consciousness can no longer effectively cooperate with the archive of the subconscious mind. Often the problem is simply that one does not want to see oneself as one really is. This leads to doing things that are not good for you or to not doing things that would be good for you.

First of all, such deviations from the inner images have an effect on the psyche, i.e. one becomes aggressive, depressive, etc. - what one actually needs, one does not receive.

On the outside, these deviations from the inner truth show themselves in the fact that one experiences failures again and again – there is not enough strength behind the "wrong way" and, moreover, walking on this way is hindered by the inner contradiction. One experiences failures again and again.

If one's behavior deviates from one's inner images for too long, the effect of the "wrong actions" continues through the emotions into the body and one becomes ill. From the nature of the illness, one can see what the cause of this illness is.

There are also a variety of warnings that the archive sends to the office when the conscious decisions are no longer in accordance with the images in the subconscious-ness: exhaustion, discouragement, burnout, failures, nightmares, faintings, illnesses, injuries, etc.

It is useful to pay attention to such warnings before the problems become even bigger …

IV 7. The healing of images

For the healing of images, one must first of all get to know them. For this purpose dream diaries and dream journeys are extremely useful. The contemplation of one's own history of illness can also be very revealing. A very thorough method to become aware of one's own problems is the awakening of one's own Kundalini – when the life force in oneself tries to flow freely again, it pushes against all inner blockages and thereby makes one aware of them …

When one's own consciously controlled behavior deviates from the inner images that express one's own actual being, a polarization into two extremes almost always arises: addict and ascetic, perpetrator and victim, and star and fan.

One image of these three pairs of images is one's own ideal and the other is one's own shadow. The projection of the shadow-image onto another person is also a problem in healing – it is not easy to recognize that the other person (who makes one's life difficult) is staging a part of one's own psyche for the common drama of these two people.

In healing, this pathological polarization has to be dissolved and the original, healthy quality has to be found again, i.e.:

- fullness (instead of the lack of the addict and the ascetic),
- power (instead of the fear of the perpetrator and the victim) and
- self-love (instead of the self-doubt of the star and the fan).

There are some aids in healing: trauma dissolution, family constellations, the principle "look, feel, embrace" and as a supporting measure also the imagination of the healed state. Another supportive measure can be singing and dancing, because in this way the life force body begins to vibrate and the inner images can slip back into their proper place. Not only dances and songs (chants) have this effect, but sometimes also mantras.

IV 8. Being in harmony with the images

The goal is to be in harmony with one's inner images. The roots of these images, i.e. the soul, the power animal, the horoscope, etc., cannot be changed – they express what one is. Therefore, only the actions decided by the waking consciousness, which are in harmony with these images, are effective.

The actions that have reached this harmony are effortless and, on the other hand, extremely effective. Magic, too, is ultimately "acting in harmony with oneself". If you do that, you don't need any rituals for magic anymore – it is enough to become aware of a wish so that its fulfillment already starts.

This inner harmony is e.g. also the basis of Zen archery: One hits thereby even things, which one cannot even see – because the harmony of the actions with the inner images leads to the fact that also telepathy and telekinesis flow effortlessly and support one's own actions.

By this harmony one finally achieves the actual magic: one simply does the impossible.

IV 9. Images in the World

Telepathy and telekinesis are the "fibers" that make up the collective subconscious. They connect all things together – just as causality connects all things together.

This makes not only magic possible, but also, for example, homeopathy, omens, oracles, Feng Shui, foreseeing the future and many other things.

V   Examples

Now that at least a large part of the properties of inner images has been shown, these principles can be described by means of examples. These examples are taken from various fields, so that the great importance of this imagery becomes palpable.

V 1.   Dreams

The following dream examples, except for the last four dreams, are all my own dreams and can therefore (except for the last four) also be considered together.

V 1. a)   The "Egyptian rule"

The Egyptians were of the opinion that if one wants to interpret the dream of a man, one must know first which deity he carries in his heart, i.e. to which deity his soul belongs. This "netjer-em-ib-i" (deity in one's own heart) is the patron deity of the person in question – the "father" or "mother" of the soul of this person. To know this deity ist important, because e.g. a quarrel means something completely different for the warlike Horus than for the midwife-goddess Thoeris …

One can also consider which horoscope the person has to be able to classify a dream. For example, I have a Saturn/Pluto-square, with Saturn in the 2nd house (home) and Pluto in the 10th house (public, authority): my parents (10th house) sent me 500km away to live with my grandparents for a year when I was a little child – and this shows up in some of my dreams.

Today, this "Egyptian rule" would probably be called a "contextual interpretation".

V 1. b)   Donkey dream

When I was four years old, I dreamed that I was a donkey living in a pasture. I am picked up by someone and taken to another pasture.

The move to another pasture is a memory of my living with my grandparents for a year instead with my parents when I was a little child.

The donkey is a farm animal – but a stubborn one. This could be a hint that I have been well-behaved, but have actually been angry inside – which is pretty much true.

V 1. c) Fire dream

When I was five, I often dreamed that my parents' house was burning down and that my grandmother was rescuing me from the burning room.

The burning parental home is a loss of support – and I found support with my grandmother.

V 1. d) Ogre dream

When I was 29, I dreamed I was sailing in a small sailing ship towards a mountainous coast – it looked like southern Italy or Greece. I climbed up the coastal slope and met an ogre – a cross between a Neanderthal man and a man-eater.

The ogre took me to a hemispherical hut. There the ogre cut me into pieces and threw me into a cauldron on a fire. Then the ogre also cut himself and threw himself into the cauldron as well (in the dream this was possible).

The ogre and I combined in the "soup" in the cauldron to form a being that is more complete than just the ogre or just me.

In this dream I experienced the integration of my shadow, that is, my repressed aggression.

Although the sweat lodge (hemispherical hut), the cauldron, and a the Scythian cannibalism ritual appear here, these symbolisms were completely unknown to me at the time.

Riding the ship symbolizes the journey to a distant place – to the other side of the psyche.

V 1. e) Isolation dream

I was in an apartment that had a completely different layout than my apartment today – but it was in approximately the same place, that is, here in this house in Alfter.

In front of my window on the sidewalk stood a man who lives here the house, whom I find very likeable, and a woman who also lives in this house, whom I find both very likeable and very interesting – although I haven't talked much with the woman yet. The two were standing there hand in hand, although that doesn't happen in real life - at least I haven't seen the two of them together yet – both also have a relationship partner.

When I saw this, strong feelings of being excluded and not belonging to thre others came up in me – and I retreated further back into my room so that the two could not see me.

This dream shows the feeling of being excluded quite directly, so there is nothing to "translate" here.

V 1. f) Mountain dream

I hiked through an area with many old, not very high mountains, in which I am often in my dreams. So far this dream hike always began at the Middle Rhine and ended finally in Italy or Portugal at the sea. This time, however, I hiked backwards, so to speak, from the mountains towards the Rhine.

The dream began with the feeling of abandonment and resignation, but then a car driver with a caravan trailer came and drove next to me a little way very slowly and looked over at me questioningly and offered to give me a lift. I wandered on, however, although the man was sympathetic to me.

A short time later I was in a village where the houses were built in such a way that one did not know where the street ended and where the houses began – a smooth transition from sidewalk to corridors to living rooms. As a result, I ended up in the living room of a family, where the children asked me if I was lost. Then they helped me find my way back.

Finally, a little further on, I sat on a low wall by the side of the road and rested. Then my ex-wife came by and was very friendly and stroked my hair.

In this dream I initially had the feeling of abandonment and exclusion, but the dream then showed me that this was not quite true. The smooth transition from living room to sidewalk is a dissolution of the inhibition to make contact.

V 1. g)   Knife dream

I dreamed that I was lying down and a half-Asian looking man was stabbing me in the back with a knife.

I suspect that I was lying funny and that this dream was triggered by the resulting pain in my back, which I also felt once the day before when I made a funny movement. The half-Asian man will be from a movie clip I saw on youtube the night before (Kwai Chang Caine from "Kung Fu"). So far this dream has no deeper roots.

However, in the dream I fought this man, wrestled with him and finally took the knife from him and drove him away.

This is, as far as I can remember, a completely new motive in my dreams – that I successfully defend myself against an attacker. Very gratifying!

V 1. h)   Murder dream

I dreamed that I had been shot and woke up from it. It was some organization or the like. I tried to hide from it and act inconspicuous, but that didn't work – it was a shot in my forehead.

"Organization" sounds like 10th house of the horoscope – there I have five planets at once … In any case, there seems to be some organization that doesn't want me to be the way I am – whatever the picture of this "organization" may have contained.

Then it looks like I don't dare to show myself as I am either – apparently out of fear of death.

The shot went into my forehead – does this refer to my Third Eye, thus to my orientation in the world … and possibly also to my adaptation to the world?

Who or what is this "organization" that has power over my life and to which I seem to submit – but unsuccessfully?

The murder in the dream happened in a house where other people have been killed before. "House" is 2nd house – that's where my Saturn is. If that should be relevant, the "organization" would have to be my Pluto, which has a square to my Saturn. And my Mars, which has a trine to my Saturn and is therefore "in the house", fears my Pluto/Neptune sextile, since it has a quincunx to both planets.

Ultimately, then, this means that my Mars is blocked by fear of death ….

To better understand the dream, I took a dream trip to the murderer from the dream:

"Hello murderer from my dream – why did you shoot me?"

"So you wouldn't do anything wrong."

"Why shoot and not poison or hang?"

"Because it's about force – that's why this murder is also a force act."

"Sounds logical. What could I have done wrong?"

"Sex."

"Hm – there's not too much 'danger' right now ... for lack of a partner ... Why this murder right now?"

"You move too much."

"What?"

"Your fire. Your kundalini. Your egoism."

"Who in me finds that threatening?"

"You will be abandoned then."

"That sounds like an old pattern, because who would be able to abandon me right now, when there's no one around?"

"Prevention."

"Hm ... I see ... and who is it in me that wants to murder my power?"

"Lovage ."

"Huh? ... Lovage has some names like 'love herb' (in English) – is the 'love stick' (German: 'Liebstöckl') the penis? The herb has digestive and cleansing effects, against flatulence, urinary tract inflammation, and against kidney grit ... it apparently promotes detachment, the throwing out of what is no longer needed ... Is there something in me that fears I might learn to say 'no' better?"

"Yes."

"Why?"

"Because then you will be abandoned."

"But I'm already abandoned, and I'm already withdrawing myself ... which, of course, confirms the theme as such – one often voluntarily does what one fears in order to prevent what one fears ... Is killing fun?"

"No."

"Do you feel like exploring alternatives with me?"

"Yes."

V 1. i) Forest dream

I was in Bad Godesberg, where I grew up. I looked for something to eat in two butcher shops – they were still open even though it was already closing time. In one kiosk I got a roll with brie and salami on it.

I walked from a dead end street, where my oldest sister's friend lived, into the forest at the Black Mountain – a path I had never walked in real life. There I met my last girlfriend's son – the two of us liked each other a lot. We discovered a rock plateau, which we climbed up.

We came through the forest to my parents' house. There was a man there who said that he had brought a cabinet made of precious cherry wood here. Out of the house moved Marion (name changed), whom I miss very much in reality. She was somehow associated with my mother. She moved a few houses away to the next crossroads – to the house where my first friend (1ˢᵗ/2ⁿᵈ school yeat) lived with a full-time foster-mother.

I went there with Marion's daughter – we two also liked each other and often played together. Jörg (my best friend) also went there. Jörg and Marion's daughter went into the house, but I stayed outside, sitting on a hill, because I was afraid that I might disturb.

I am in Godesberg – a childhood theme.

I want to eat meat – I need strength, assertiveness.

I find a sausage/brie roll – cheese has something maternal-safe because it is made from milk. Plus, brie is "soft cheese."

I go through an unfamiliar dead end – new paths …

I go to the forest – the area of life force.

The forest at Black Mountain is threatening and gloomy (even in reality) – I venture into unknown territory.

I meet the son of my last girlfriend – I protect someone … or is it myself as little Harry? Probably both …

We find a rocky plateau (which in reality is not there) – firm foundation, foresight, clarity …

However, the rock plateau was not public, but private terrain – actually we were not allowed to be there, so we do something semi-forbidden.

We come to my parents' house – a childhood theme.

A man brings a cherry wood cabinet – cherry wood is precious, a cabinet keeps something, man = father?; does my father bring us or me something valuable?

Marion comes out of the house or rather I know that she has left the house – abandonment trauma; the girlfriend is equal to my mother … (Marion has moved away from Alfter).

The house of my first school friend who lived with a kind of "foster-grandmother" because the mother was a single parent (she lived 10km away and saw her child from time to time) – an analogy to my year with my grandparents at the age of 1.5 - 2.5 years.

Marion is moving there – I also analogized her to my grandmother.

I accompany Marion's daughter to her new apartment – to see Marion?

Jörg accompanies me there – is this the "successful man", the "man of the woman I would like to be close to"? Then he would be a mixture of my father and my eldest sister and the rather dominant men with whom the women are almost always with, with whom I am friends.

Jörg goes to Marion's house with Marion's daughter – he has the contact that I don't have …

I stay sitting outside because I fear being annoying or intrusive – this is my survival strategy … and since I have almost only dealt with women who have been raped, my own initiatives are often vehemently rejected by them or perceived as a massive violation – meanwhile my reticence and my fear of disturbing has probably become a problem in encounters itself …

Obviously I am still looking for security with my mother and with my grandmother. And I obviously mix this search for security with my relationships, where, after all, this quality cannot be found – a relationship is something different from a child-mother relationship …

V 1. j) Wizard dream

I have dreamed of having been first to a wizard and then to a sorceress who advised me – the advice of the sorceress suited me better. Unfortunately, I don't remember what they told me.

It seems that I got a new kind of dream: a wise person helping me. Obviously something fundamental is changing in my psyche.

V 1. k) Spock dream

Mr. Spock is lying dead on a kind of table. A faceless man standing near the foot of this table has killed him. Captain Kirk comes into the room and recognizes the situation. The man is armed with a saber. Kirk takes the saber, which is lying on the stretcher to the left of Spock, and says to the dead Spock, "You permit?" Kirk and the man fight. Finally, Kirk kills the man by cutting off both of his feet. This causes something to fall out of Spock so that he comes back to life.

I was called "Spock" for a while in school because of the way I think. So I assume that in the dream I am mainly Spock – even though all dream motifs are part of

46

myself, of course.

I know the cutting off of the feet from the Germanic Tyr-myth: The feet, hands and head of the summer god Tyr were cut off by the winter god Loki in autumn – there are also other variants of the myth, where e.g. only one hand is cut off. The saber next to Spock will therefore be the sword of Tyr. I have quite a close connection to Tyr – he and his successor Baldur are the German equivalent to my patron deity Osiris.

The "rebirth" of Spock is reminiscent of my favorite fairy tale, "Snow White," in which Snow White reawakens when the poisonous apple bite falls out of her throat. Snow White is a fairy tale variation of Freya, the goddess of rebirth, who also gave rebirth to Tyr.

The dream is apparently about rebirth. The rebirth is not brought about by the stumbling of a pallbearer, as in "Snow White," but by the victory of Kirk against the faceless man. In the Germans, too, Tyr is victorious against Loki in the spring.

Kirk seems to be the victorious Tyr. Is he my strength, my fighting spirit, my willingness to conflict? … My will?

Spock is apparently the largely emotionless mind – the observing "researcher Harry" who does not want anything? Then this dream would represent the integration of wanting and fighting in me.

Who is the faceless man who killed Spock? Since I can barely see him, I can't say much there – so I asked him with the help of a dream journey:

"Hello faceless man from my dream – who are you?"
"You."
"What part of me?"
"Your fear."
"My fear of what?"
"Of you, of your power."
"So far I have already realized that from the dream. Can you tell me something else that I am not yet aware of?"
"No, because that's not what it's about."
"What is it about?"
"About your power. Integrate it."
"How?"
"Do."
"What?"
"Whatever you feel like doing."
"Anything? Composing, sex, wandering, whatever? Or is there something impor-tant?"
"Anything that has to do with other people."
"So 'resting in myself,' sex, setting boundaries, love, conversation, making contact,

and the like?"

"Yes – especially saying 'no' without fear."

"No fear of abandonment?"

"Yes, and no fear of homelessness and starvation – but you've already cured those."

"Is there a concrete step I could take to further this integration?"

"Don't be moralistic. Don't think too much about what might be. Follow the desire."

"Hmm ... isn't that one-sided?"

"You're one-sided now – by doing these things, you'll come back more into balance."

"Hmm, yes, you can look at it that way, I understand that. ... Is there anything else you could tell me about this?"

"No – not now."

"Thank you."

"Sure."

"Ho!"

V 1. l) England dream

I am walking through a small English town consisting mainly of a main street – probably in north central England. The record "Abbey Road" by the Beatles, which has just been released, can be heard – so it must be 1969, since this record was released on 9/26/1969.

I see the word "Maxwell" which probably refers to the third song on this record titled "Maxwell's Silver Hammer" which describes the student Maxwell who kills three people because they did something he didn't like.

Next, I am in a house and see a man of uncertain age who is uncomfortable but who is hiding this. Then I see him in a bathroom in a shower. He is afraid that someone might come into the room and see him – not because he is naked, but because he is secretly turning to fire, which he doesn't want anyone to know. First his contours, especially his face, become blurred, his color changing at first to the milky white with a slight blue sheen of the life force, and then gradually becoming more fiery – there are no flames to be seen, however, but they can be felt.

The man has a high inner pressure to become fire, but does not want this to be noticed – he has this problem in bed while sleeping and on other occasions.

Maxwell could be a symbol for repressed aggression or for unrestrained aggression. This non-integrated aggression is well known to me. It shows itself among other things in my occasional inner aggression pictures.

In 1969 I was 13 years old, but I don't think that has any meaning – or does it refer to a blocked beginning of my puberty?

What about north central England? I've only been to England once so far, and I haven't really experienced anything special in central England.

The perception of the life force body and the fire refer quite certainly to the Kundalini.

Why is the man afraid to show his "fire"? The man is probably me and the fire is not only my kundalini but also my will.

Does being naked in the shower refer to sexuality?

This dream seems to me to be an addition to the dream of yesterday: Yesterday the integration of the emotion of Captain Kirk into the cool mind of Mr. Spock, and today the perception of the feared and repressed and therefore also destructive (Maxwell's murders) wanting-fire and its presumably hoped-for integration.

So I ask the fire-man in a short dream journey:

"Fire-man – do you want to tell me anything else about this dream?"
"It is so exhausting ..."
"What is exhausting?"
"Not being what I am."
"Why aren't you being what you are?"
"Fear."
"Of what?"
"Mom."
"Hmm ... what about her?"
"How am I supposed to live without her?"
"Hm ... how old are you?"
"Three."
"Have you noticed that you and I, that is Harry, are now 63 years old?"
"No."
"Can you see it?"
"Yes."
"Can you tell what you need so you can be yourself again?"
"Love."
"From whom?"
"From you."
"Love for little Harry? ... Self-love?"
"Yes."
"I feel that there is not yet as much self-love as there could be, but I can take you in my arms – will you?"
"Yes."

I do. I hold the three-year-old child who is also the fire-man. He slumps down all at once. I sit down so that I can continue to hold him in my arms. He begins to twitch ... I just continue to hold him. He has collapsed – I think it was this holding up, this wanting to hide.

There's a lot going on inside him ... it goes on for quite a while ... I can see he's getting 'softer' ...

I think we should just sit here together for a while and just let happen what wants to happen ...

V 1. m) Symbol dream

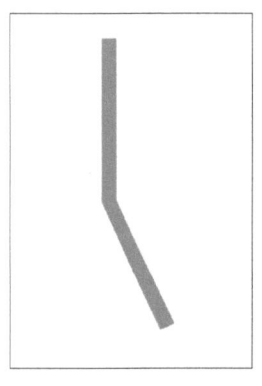

I dreamed tonight of a geometric shape – a glowing red-orange angle of about 30°. This angle moved from right to left – apparently on a spherical surface, so that it came back into the picture from the right. Sometimes this angle also seemed like an opening through which I can look into the glow inside a sphere.

I concentrated on this angle in the dream and returned to it again and again – about 8-10 times. A few days ago I have dreamed about this angle, too – about 15-20 times in a row.

The red glow of this angle indicates that it is about power – about the Kundalini?

What is the angle? An astrological half-sextile? Then it would be about further development. Or is it a fraction? It actually looked too tensionless, organic and right for a fraction.

What is the sphere? My root chakra? My life force body?

What is this kinked line? My sushumna, that is, the central life force canal, obstructed by something?

The constant repetition of the dream and also the abstract symbolism suggest that it is something important and possibly also something rhythmic.

V 1. n)   Moscow dream

I traveled to Moscow by train because a woman who lives there invited me there. I got off at a suburban train station in the northwest of Moscow and walked along a country road or highway to the suburb of Moscow. Then it struck me that I can't remember the woman's name and I don't have her address with me.

I turned off at a highway entrance and came to a kind of horseshoe-shaped hill house. Inside, a path gradually went up in switchbacks to the highest point. The apartments were in the hill itself – the doors facing to the inner side of the horseshoe-hill and the windows facing outward. This village building had about four floors and a total of probably a little more than 50 apartments – perhaps the whole thing was still a little higher and larger as I could see.

I realized in the dream that I had to come here, but that I was afraid to meet the woman. I remembered that the woman is quite plump.

I arrive at the garden gate at the opening of the horseshoe-shaped hill and go inside. A woman to my right greets me with my name. I see two plump women to my right in front, but the one who invited me is not there.

I pass a window to my right. There a woman and a man are in bed with each other and either he is tickling her or they are having sex with each other. It becomes clear to me that people here live free love in open relationships.

I walk up the serpentines to the top of the house hill. From the outside it looks more like a hill than a house – from the inside, shaped like the inside of a horseshoe, it looks more like a house or a "three-quarters circle of houses". I look around me and think that now I can walk back again and I am relieved.

But already after a few meters it becomes dark and I slip at the edge of the way. I try to find my footing and accidentally pull a man who was walking in front of me down the slope with me. Two floors down we come to a stop and are both unhurt. There is a brief grumbling of discontent between us, but I then realize that I was the one who caused it.

I continue all the way down and then leave the hill village.

It's about the relationship between me and a woman. Since the woman with whom I last spent a night lives in the very east of Germany in a lonely area ("suburb of Moscow"), she will probably be meant.

She invites me and I am afraid to come, but I come anyway. This corresponds to her call yesterday, to which I did not answer. She also thinks the principle of free love is good – that also fits. Moreover, ZEGG, a village where people live like this, is near Berlin, that is, in the East.

In this dream I am unintentionally dragging a man down a slope with me. Another girlfriend of mine fell in love with a man I'm friends with – that must have been the man I accidentally dragged down the slope with me. I guess that was a symbol that I don't know what's going to happen with me and this girlfriend, nor what's going to happen with me and this friend. But, after all, no grudge remained between me and this man in the dream.

The central theme of the dream is probably that I am looking for something that is right, important and essential and that I don't have in my current encounters – not that they are wrong, but just not really 'in touch with the heart of life', to put it more poetically. That's why I don't know what I want with the 'woman from the East'.

V 1. o) Panther dream

I dreamed of a rather dark hallway in a large public building or similar, in which I was standing and from the right a rather dark and quite passive looking man rode past me on a giant cat, resembling a black panther, to the left through a kind of door without door wings, behind which the hallway continued. The panther did scare me a bit, but I wasn't really afraid of it either.

A corridor is a fixed path, the rider is probably myself, the "panther-cat" is power, the "gate" is a transition, to the left is the past. So my power is flowing back along a corridor through a gate to an old state – this sounds very much like my kundalini, which has arrived in a new realm through one of the intermediate chakras.

V 1. p) Trapeze dream

I have been trapped in a room by a middle aged woman. She has made two pressed chipboards out of wood chips, which are somehow parts of me. One has the shape of an elongated trapezoid and represents my body; on it is a second trapezoid with two holes, representing my head with my eyes; the second board stands at right angles behind it so that the first board can stand upright. The woman has banished a part of my life force into this board, which has thus become a kind of Woodoo doll of me. The possession of this wooden figure gives her power over me.

She threatens to kill me with the help of this figure or the like. I suddenly make the decision to banish my life force from this figure, so that it is only a wooden figure and the woman then has no more power over me. I stretch out both arms in a complex gesture, in which both arms and hands do something different, against the wooden figure and shout loudly two words, which were approximately "Kramparlik krilikril!"

- the sound of these words, which were completely unknown to me, was very hard and rough, they reminded me a bit of the Orc language from the 'Lord of the Rings'.

Since I actually physically shouted these words out loud, I woke up from it. My first, slightly amused thought was what someone who had also been here in my room would have thought when I shouted such words in my sleep.

A middle aged woman possesses parts of me and therefore has power over me and uses them to harm me. I want to take these parts (life force) away from her, but am not sure in the dream if I will succeed.

Why a wooden figure? And why trapezoids? The figure is most reminiscent of the pillars from the temples of Göbekli Tepe (10,000 BC), which represent the ancestors and were 'stone totem poles'. But why? Because these parts of me have been in the possession of this woman for a long time? Is this my mother?

Why pressed chipboard and not grown wood? Apparently there has been some destruction and from the rubble after this destruction the abstract, wooden figure has been made. Sounds like the old argument with my mother. Should I now have regained contact with these old events on the dream level? That would be ingenious, because then I can change something about it now.

And I tried to get back my own life(-force).

V 1. q) Murderer dream

A man is not a murderer, but almost. He sits in the front left and steers the car. I sit in the back left of the car and duck down as low as I can; there are others in the car – the man threatens them and forces them out with a gun; when they are outside, I hear gunshots.

The whole thing takes place in Bad Godesberg in front of the railroad underpass that connects to Bahnhofstraße. You can't go there by car at all, but I associate this place with a threat made against his son by the father of the ex-husband of the woman for whom I made a dream trip yesterday.

The man uses violence against others. I know about it. I seem to be a woman. The man and I are lying together in a bed.

The man says to me, "You won't tell, because I will always find you – with your profession, you can't live by word of mouth alone, you have to be on the Internet."

I walk through a dark, wide street; I cross an intersection; the apartment of me and the man is behind me on the left; he could watch me through the window and recognize me by the way I hesitate in my movement and then don't go to the house, but keep walking. He would see my fear if he looked out of the window and recognize me by it.

I walk across a two-lane, unlit avenue; houses on the right, open space on the left, like a park meadow like Poppelsdorfer Allee in Bonn; I cross the street, a car comes from the right in front, I quickly walk all the way across the street; this was not dangerous, but careless.

I am now on the path at the edge of the lawn in the middle of the tree-lined road; there is a construction site: holes in the ground, barriers, a living container open at the front in which about four construction workers are sitting – feels like a living community. A woman clings to me, I do not know her, I send her away, she is afraid – of the man who also threatens me? I seem to be a man again now; the four or so men come out of the container and ask what's going on; I say that I don't know the woman; they are astonished, but believe me; the woman is fleeing from something.

The basic feeling is of being threatened as a woman – me as a woman or the woman clinging to me. But there is no sexual threat apparent.

The threat is massive and I cannot escape it – I duck, I flee, I try not to be seen. I am partially in the man's grip – same bed, I am in his car.

The construction worker, who is well-disposed towards me, cannot help me. A construction site is a place where something is being changed. What? Something in the earth, thus something old. So a healing? On a meadow in the city – more liveliness?

Bonn and Bad Godesberg are the places where I lived for a long time, but not the woman for whom I made the dream journey. Only the association to her ex-husband and his father speaks for the fact that the dream could have something to do with her.

It is night – so I am in my subconscious, i.e. in the area where I can also find hidden things.

What is this being threatened by a despotic man? I inwardly ask the man who he is.

He says very loudly, "You!"
"What do you want?"
"You!"
"And what do you want to do?"
"To be free! To be free! To be free!"
At this, I have images of him smashing things – he is angry because he is being held captive.
I ask him inwardly, "Who imprisoned you?"
"Who did – you!"
"Why?"
"Fear."
"Of what?"
"Of your power?"

"What am I afraid of?"
"Abandonment."
"By whom?"
"By everyone."
"Where did it start?"
"With your mother."
"Does that mean that you are my anger at having been prevented from doing what I want?"
"Yes."
"And now you want to use power to gain your freedom?"
"No one shall hinder me anymore!"

This looks like an issue that belongs to me and not to the woman, who I counseled yesterday. It could be, of course, that the woman knows a similar theme and that the dream journey to her theme has opened the door in me to the corresponding theme. This would also explain the association with the father of her ex-husband.

I ask the man from the dream about this:

"Hello, man – is there any connection to the woman for whom I made the dream journey?"
"Same theme ... or at least very similar: blocked Mars ..."
"What can I do to heal my Mars?"
"Dance."
"Just dance?"
"Yes."
"Hm ... and what could the woman do to the healing of her Mars?"
"Sex. And no more fear of punishment from the world, no more fear of herself, of her power."
"Thank you."

V 1. r) Ship dream

I have packed my about 15 most important books on magic and the like and am flying somewhere by plane. The plane has to make an emergency landing at sea. It is unclear for a long time whether someone rescues us, although distress calls and the position information have been sent out. I myself call relatives with a borrowed cell phone. A younger man says that I and someone else have received an entry in Wikipedia. I think of a series of articles/chapters for a book that I have written/outlined.
Finally, a large cargo ship comes and takes us in. We all can only take our carry-on

luggage, but not our suitcases. So I lose my magic books. It's my turn to board the ship at the end, and I hold on to a ship's rope, which pulls me up to the deck. On the ship, the rescued are sitting at a large U-shaped row of tables on deck.

The land is close by, which amazes me. I disembark with the others. I meet a few people among the rescued, whom I know loosely here from Alfterm where I live – especially from the organic food store that I ran with others for 20 years. I borrow a cell phone and call someone to pick me up. Someone asks if it's my grandma. I answer that it is my aunt – it is my godmother, my mother's sister.

It is apparently about magic (books). I'm writing the chapter outlines for real book right now, too ("Living Magic"). The entry in Wikipedia probably refers to Frater U.D. and me, since we are partly working on a book project together with my friend Jörg and my magic teacher Axel.

My godmother and my grandmother refer to my childhood – I spent a year with my grandparents and my godmother lived with my parents for some years. Is there a connection there with the argument with my mother? That I contact relatives is very unusual for me – and also that I ask them for help.

It seems to be about magic and about my relatives (grandma, godmother; mother?).

The ship seems very heavy, large, massive and sturdy. The U-shaped table on the deck has something of a ritual.

Since I am flying on the plane, I seem to want to go far with my magic (about 15 books) – the entry of me and probably Frater U.D. in Wikipedia speaks for this. However, this plan obviously fails, because the plane has to ditch. This failure is life-threatening, since it is unclear whether help comes before the airplane sinks.

I want to achieve something by magic – is the rising of the plane also the rising of the Kundalini? It is conceivable, but uncertain …

I call my relatives and receive help from them – is this the big ship? Is that my mother?

There is no ladder or the like where I can comfortably climb up to the deck, but I am pulled up by a rope. So I can't get to my relatives independently, but only by their help. The U-shaped row of tables looks like a family reunion.

I seem to have to give up magic for admission into the circle of relatives. This is actually not so in reality – nobody really understands what I am doing, but nobody says anything against it. Is "magic" therefore a symbol for my independence, which I gave up at that quarrel at the age of three? I know the "me or magic" from my first relationship though – at that time I actually sold all my magic books because my girlfriend would have left me otherwise.

V 1. s) Tyr dream

Tonight I half woke up because I was saying the words "son bodn" to myself and felt a "soft" pulsating alternately left and right in my chest – with the frequency of about 1Hz. It felt a bit like female breasts. I realized while still half asleep that this was Ida and Pingala.

In Old Norse, "son" means "son" and "bodn" means "barrel." These are two of the three ritual vessels for the mead potion. The third vessel is named "Odrrörir", meaning "one who awakens ecstasy". The third vessel is the drinking horn of the former sungod-godfather Tyr, the other two vessels are the drinking horns of his two twin sons ("Alcis").

Apparently I have equated in me Tyr and his two Alcis sons to the Sushumna as well as Ida and Pingala.

Did I direct the life-force in this dream as in Yoga from Ida and Pingala into the central Sushumna?

V 1. t) Tundra dream

I was on the southern edge of the Siberian tundra in a loose spruce forest. Someone (a man?) had chopped down a rather dry spruce and set it on fire, dragging it under some other dry spruces so that the fire spread to them. I saw that I had no way to extinguish the fire, so I fled through the dry grass and loose spruce trees – I was also a bit afraid of the "fire man" (I didn't see his face, but it felt like a man). Then I came to a path that led down into a valley. There were others running down into the valley there – about three men between the ages of 20-28. They ran individually and partly overtook me.

There I probably dreamed of my Kundalini fire, which ignited and that I apparently also fear.

Why did the man have to carry the fire to the other spruces? Is this an image of the fire breathing by which I try to awaken the Kundalini?

Why are there the young men fleeing from the fire? Because at their age I was afraid of the Kundalini?

And why tundra? Siberian shaman magic? Probably Russia means here approximately "unknown and tending dangerous stranger" and thus designates my shadow, thus the repressed part of my psyche.

In the valley was no forest, thus that was a suitable escape place – there were also some small towns.

V 1. u) Moon dream

I was on a moon orbiting a planet far from our solar system. There everything was completely different than on earth – among other things there were rivers of light. On one of these rivers I took an acquaintance of mine in a kind of rowboat up-river to my son.

The whole scenery was inly a very little "earthy" – more like the clairvoyantly perceived landscape of life force.

The river trip could refer specifically to a friend who wants to meet my son, who lives upriver from me.

From the scenery a completely crazy dream – it must look similar on LSD trips …

V 1. v) Eulenburg dream

The dream consisted of only one sentence: *"I'm going to get the Eulenburg back!"*

The Eulenburg is the castle Yladia ("Eulen-Aue-Burg" = "castle in the owl-meadow") near the town Eylau ("Eulen-Aue" = "owl-meadow") in West Prussia, which my ancestor Arnulph von Eylenstein ("Eilenstein" = "Eylenstein" = "owl-stone") founded Anno 1326 for the knights of the Teutonic Order. In the dream, "Burg" referred to my parents' house, which now belongs to my brother and where he lives together with his family and my mother.

Obviously, something in me has decided to stop sacrificing all my possessions "for the sake of dear peace" and to return to my power.

- - -

V 1. w) City dream

This dream, and also the three that follow, are not mine, but those of a woman. The dreams of this woman are much longer and contain much more details then my own dreams.

It is daytime, the sky is hazy but bright.

day: It is about something conscious.
hazy: It is probably not only hazy of the weather, but also of the mood.

I walk down a sidewalk along a wall of houses, in some city. They are plain dark gray row houses without front yards to my left, the front doors bordering directly on the sidewalk.

desolate civilization: presumably external forms that slow down the joy of living

I walk past an obviously abandoned house, the steps to the entrance are weathered, the door is open and yawns like a dark hole. In the house entrance are torn off doorbell signs but no names. I walk past it, but then stop and walk backwards to the entrance again. Something draws me magically, my curiosity is aroused.

house: often one's own body
no name tags: anonymity – one is meaningless
no doorbell: no contact possibilities – isolation
going to the house: wanting to understand something – oneself

I see a figure standing in the darkness of the hallway, looking at me. Although I cannot recognize the face clearly, I feel invited to enter.
The young man beckons me to go with him and walks through a narrow, half-buried door into daylight. He pushes aside beams and green vegetation that has grown over the opening, so that I can follow him.

the man is "familiar with the place" – he's a part of the psyche.
half-buried door: here begins a part of the psyche that is at most still half-conscious
growth: there is still a rest of life there

We step into a kind of courtyard, until I realize that it must once have been a stately living room, with shallow steps to several levels as well as a huge brick fireplace at the end. Almost everything has been overgrown by plants or covered with bright green moss, which looks even more intense on the dark gray stone.

living room: center
has become courtyard: ceiling gone = unprotected
fireplace: fire in the body = kundalini
moss: only slightly organized life force

As my eyes adjust to the sparse light, I see a young, brown-haired man about my age looking up at me as if he had been waiting for me. He resembles the Canadian actor Ryan Reynolds, quite attractive. Although I don't know him, I seem to be familiar with him. He leads me into the hall of the house.

already the second young man: are relationships a relevant topic?

The walls are gray and dark, rubble lies around and plants have grown inside the

59

dilapidated building. I put my head back and look up, seeing a perforated roof several stories above me through which some daylight comes in. Several stone staircases wind their way up, everything is gray, dark and almost devoid of color except for the green of plants that have gradually reclaimed the house. From the inside, the building is much larger and more winding than the narrow wall of the house had suggested from the outside.

the house is larger from the inside than it looks from the outside: the grandeur (and former wealth?) of the interior is hidden
plants: hope?

It must have been a very modern living room of the 60s/70s. The roof is almost completely gone, so now it looks like a courtyard. The aura is mystical and fascinating. Especially the big fireplace, which surely hasn't seen a fire for years, has a strong attraction for me. We linger briefly so that I can let the atmosphere take effect on me.

60s/70s: Does the time about 50 years ago play a role? Own age? Parents?
the fascination of the fireplace confirms its interpretation as Kundalini aspect
mystical, fascinating: astrologically Neptune and Uranus – do they play a role?

It almost has the impression of a temple complex in the jungle ... mysterious.

temple complex: Neptune again ...

The man beckons again to follow him and enters the interior of the building through a wide terrace door. We walk up the stairs and look into various rooms, all of which are almost completely overgrown. I hardly recognize individual objects, only contours and shadows in dark gray covered with green moss.

visiting a house: looking at one's own body?

He seems pleased to show me the whole house. Excitedly, he leads me from one room to the next, up and up. It seems as if the building belongs to him or rather as if he commands over it. Like over an abandoned kingdom.

joy: Was it about time to see the hidden again? Was this missing in real life? Uranus and Neptune – so pep and mystery?
The dream gives the impression of finding again something lost or forgotten – probably another way of life.
Is it a man who shows her the rooms, because the "man-role" allows something that the "woman-role" forbids?

He shows me in the upper floors another kind of courtyard under the open sky,

60

again full of plants all around and another fireplace, a bit smaller than the first one, but not less imposing made of gray stone.

upper floors: heart chakra or throat chakra
fireplace: connection to the Kundalini fire
a lot of hidden plants in a house ruin: Does this woman not live all the life that is in her? Wrong profession? Wrong life- circumstances? Blocking herself?

I see an old man sitting on the stone slab in front of it, leaning on a walking stick, wearing an baseball cap. I don't know him and he doesn't seem to take any notice of us, but looks absently but peacefully into the interior of the empty fireplace. My companion does not seem surprised to see him here. He leads me further up the weathered stairs and when we reach the top it becomes brighter and also more modern.

old man: wisdom, knowledge
he does not react: still inaccessible, not integrated
This dream seems to be to a large part about the characteristics of men – is "masculinity" or similar needed?

We enter a kind of loft; here the walls are still plastered white, the floor of gray tiles, pale sunlight penetrates. The mystical, temple-like atmosphere of the lower part of the building does not exist here. It rather gives the impression of an abandoned school or train station building. Serviceable and modern, but abandoned. For the first time I notice graffiti on the walls; plaster and glass splinters crunch under my feet.

loft: the head, third eye, mind
no temple atmosphere: Uranus and Neptune have not been integrated into the head, i.e. into the rational world view. Is this the basic problem? Maybe this woman functions well in normal life or in her profession, but is longing for more alifeness and life force ("plants") in her life.
station/school atmosphere: life-hostile objectivity
graffities: thoughts, but also "revolutionary impudence", maladjustment or similar, also again Uranus = Does this woman want to speak upfront her mind to some people – maybe her parents or her superiors? Maybe she has been to dutifully and submissive?
splinter: destruction in former times
more modern: The head/Mercury was used longer than the heart or Uranus/Neptun – maybe until today.

I hear voices of other people who obviously live here. To my left is the entrance to a collective toilet, the door unhooked and leaning against the wall. I see three enclosed toilet stalls in white, the kind you see in public buildings. Here, too, there are sprayed structures on the wall. I walk towards the leftmost toilet door as a young blonde woman approaches from behind and pushes past me. She grabs the door handle and looks at me with a challenging grin. She is pierced on the chin, has a capie on her head, wears skater clothes and looks like she lives on the street. I don't know her and have no other contact with people like her. The young woman says something to annoy me, albeit smiling. I say something back and she has to laugh. We grin at each other and feel familiar now. Friendly. We understand each other.

cheekiness, piercing, skaters, grinning, living on the street: Counterpoint to the matter-of-factness, to the destroyed "temples". This seems to be a part that is not lived – but the woman, who dreamt this, finds pleasure in it and joins in.

toilet: demarcation, being able to say "no" – what is missing to be whole

I leave the toilet and enter the loft, it is now sunlit and very spacious. The impression of the decaying building fades. It seems like a secret place where people have gathered to form a shared apartment. Besides the woman, I dimly see another man and a teenage boy with dark blond curls, slightly overweight and very mischievous. I lean against the counter of a kitchen island that stands in the middle of the loft. The others join me. The young man who brought me over somehow seems to be the leader (protector?) of the group.

people in the loft: community of outcasts, the woman (who dreamed this) is not alone with her desires to be different

I feel comfortable with these people. It seems as if they are outcasts of society, marginal inhabitants of the bourgeois world in an abandoned building. Strangely, a feeling of belonging to the group flows through me. At the same time melancholy arises, I have to go again and leave these people who are strange to me and at the same time familiar. I write my phone number on a piece of paper lying on the counter. The boy stands on tiptoe next to it and looks curiously at the sheet. We will exchange numbers so we can stay in touch.

belonging/feeling sorry: wanting to belong to them, but not knowing how
telephone numbers: but still keeping in touch

It seems that this woman wants to change her life – she probably is imprisoned in her profession, in her parent's attitude to life and the like. She is not as "colorful" in her "real life" as she really is inside.

V 1. x) Shoe dream

This dream comes from the same woman as the previous dream.

I enter a Deichmann shoe store together with my husband. Inside it is illuminated with yellowish light and covered with a dark gray carpet. I vaguely perceive other customers and muffled murmurs of voices.

shoes: contact with the earth?
astrology: shoes = feet = 12th house = contact with the whole world?
with husband: relationship issue?

I look straight ahead and see several models displayed on a stack of shoe boxes. Enthusiastically, I discover a pair of blue ankle boots and light brown boots with a beautiful rounded shape and only a little heel. Exactly such boots I am always desperately looking for!

That sounds more like the 2nd house: fitting clothes.

Buying shoes has not necessarily been my favorite activity since my teenage years. Due to my large feet, it was always problematic to find suitable shoes that also look at least reasonably good. Especially as a teenager I found it terrible never to be able to wear "cool" shoes like the others in my class. As if I was handicapped because of my size.
So I'm all the happier and relieved to discover these models. And the light brown boots are also size 42 – I can hardly believe my luck!
Immediately I put on the right boot and must determine to my astonishment that he is at least 3 sizes too big. I really do not know that. Too small, yes. But too big?

The search for something suitable, which also makes outward "impression" … This sounds as if this woman is yearning for acceptance just as she is.

I take it off again and look in the right part of the store, whether there are other sizes? Slowly I walk past the shelves with the shoes on display, here there seems to be only single pairs in the sale. My husband trots silently behind me. Slowly the suspicion arises in me that the pair of boots is no longer available in my size. A neat, dark-haired saleswoman in her mid-20s walks past us. I approach her and she tells me that the boot is no longer available in any other size, but that she could show me another model. I feel bitter disappointment.

right: this direction symbolizes the future – is there a solution?
man trots behind: Does he want something else?

She runs away and comes back with a large cardboard box. The three of us kneel down on the scratchy gray carpet. She opens the box and I see vaguely light green boots. I don't like the color. These are not the boots I wanted so badly.

The saleswoman also has a clear plastic box with her and pokes a hole in the plastic on top with her dark red painted fingernails. She rips open the plastic and pulls out a huge piece of meat, the size of a German shepherd dog. She spreads a piece of plastic wrap on the floor in front of us, then lays the big piece of raw meat on it in front of me.

I think I understand that the boots are made of this material. I look down at the meat, streaked with white fat, and stroke the moist surface, regretfully and almost tenderly. Part of the piece has gotten next to the plastic, leaving a grease stain on the carpet. I wonder what kind of animal it was.

I look to my husband kneeling beside me and hear myself say, "That's what we were talking about. The prices to pay for everything."

The saleswoman seems unconcerned and waiting, but I feel sadness and somehow regret. I don't want a living being to die for my shoes. I sigh, because I realize at the same time that from now on it will be even more difficult for me to find suitable shoes that have been created without sacrifice.

red painted fingernails: blood?

killing animal for leather shoes: is the "healthy aggression" missing here?

talking with her husband about the topic: "healthy aggression", i.e. constructive quarrel and selfishness in the relationship?

Is the dead animal (meat) a symbol of the imprisonment of her own life force? Has she imprisoned it herself in order to look more "cool" and to be accepted by others? This would be the same meaning as the ruined house in the last dream in which the wild growing plants are some sort of repressed and partly hidden life force of this woman.

V 1. y) City dream

This dream originates from the same acquaintance:

A work situation in my office: my colleague M. from accounting enters the room and pushes several pieces of paper into my hand – new work instruction from the USA, please implement immediately – and rushes out again. It is about the fact that all product pictures, which were provided after newest US guidelines in the dimensions are to be changed and stored differently. Since I was in charge of the project (in reality) and had to fill the database with the mass of photos, I briefly do an overview in my head and come to the conclusion that this means a huge effort and does not make sense from several aspects.

Having to do nonsensical and superfluous work: the general feeling of life?

I am indignant and excited, this can't be true! Just a note from the USA and I am supposed to do this? My colleague T. turns to me and says that if this comes from the "Interna" list, it would be correct, a committee would have passed it and that is the way it is. I am stunned and upset, resistance stirs in me.

I stand in the center of the office and explain to my colleagues present why this is nonsense, it is an incomprehensible expenditure and it results in only disadvantages for us! Nobody really reacts, they seem disinterested, it's not their problem. Even my supervisor M. continues to look at his screen as if I were just air. Somehow I can't express myself, the message doesn't get through.

helplessness: "Nobody hears me! No one helps me!" ... the child left alone? The will of the child supressed by it's parents?

So I give a concrete example and get more and more upset, turn to my colleague E. from my team and ask him to confirm this, he is also a professional. But E. also turns his back on me and looks at his screen. I step closer to him, talk to him. Why doesn't he answer? He should only confirm the statement! But he seems almost amused by my efforts. I become more and more hysterical, now I even yell at him. I am his superior, he should take a stand. It feels awful to play out the hierarchy; I shy away from that in reality, too. But in the dream I have no choice and in my desperation I come up with the "I boss – you obey" number.

The problem of "not being seen" is obvious. This is probably related to the "house dream", in which the collapse of the "official, bourgeois order" and the longing for a freer, more "rebellious" life is shown.

The hysteria corresponds to the outsiders from the house-dream.

However, that doesn't pull either, he remains stubborn and ignores me. The others in the office are also unimpressed by my outburst of rage and continue to work in silence. So I turn to M. again and ask him to talk to me in private. Together we leave the office and step into the hallway.

However, it is not the hallway of my company, but looks more like the hallway of an American school. Dark brown clinker on the walls and light gray, mirror-like linoleum flooring. It vaguely reminds me of my high school days.

Perhaps the theme of "discipline versus liveliness" was also present in the school.

I tell M. that he has now seen how difficult it is to work with E., but he seems unim-pressed. I start crying with helplessness, tell him that my motivation tends towards 0 due to exactly such situations and that I lose any motivation. Now he suddenly reacts and seems angry: "Of course that can't be!" It is as if he is only now awakening to life and noticing me at all. He now also seems upset and says we have to draw conse-quences with regard to E.'s behavior and discuss the matter on another level.

Apparently only functioning counts – this is probably also the basic problem, since this corresponds to "not being seen".

He marches across the hall and beckons me to follow him. We walk through a wide door and enter a large, bright room, also covered with gray linoleum. The walls are white, there are light wooden tables and benches around where people sit and talk in a murmur, several large houseplants in pots obscure the view of details. Although I do not know the room, I am sure that it is a teacher's room. Overall, it seems somewhat sparse and utilitarian, having a Scandinavian look.

Unsure of where to put myself, I stand around, it reminds me of the awe I used to have when I was allowed to enter the sacred refuge of the teachers, otherwise I had to stand in front of the door. I feel queasy, somehow this is getting out of hand. I just wanted to be heard and that I don't have to implement a project without resistance, which makes no sense. What are they going to do with E.? Have I exaggerated? I get a bad conscience towards him.

Torn between adaptation and rebellion …

Someone tells me to go into another room. It resembles the first one, with light wooden benches lining the walls, almost a bit like the gym used to be. I take a feather bed from the bench and cover it with lilac bedding. With the thick bedding under my arm, I walk on into a new, smaller room. Daylight shines in from a window on the left. The room is completely filled with a glass cylinder that sinks a bit into the floor. Below is a round white mattress filling the cylinder.

gym: sports, physical activity – possibly sex?
glass cylinder: something is "exhibited" publicly
mattress in the glass cylinder: is sex being exhibited here?

Now I stand in the tube on the mattress and look up, up the panes. Actually, it's not that uncomfortable with the bedding in here.

My former supervisor F. from my old company enters the room and looks through the glass, I look up at him. He says something about it being quite thick glass and confirms my impression of a prison. I don't know how I got in there, but I can't get out of this "aquarium" by myself, but at least it's comfortable in here.

glass prison: being isolated – a consequence of "not being seen" … (see "The Wall" by Pink Floyd)

former supervisor: the story started early – probably in the family of origin and then continued through school into profession …

isolated, but safe … probably this has been for the most time of her life her general solution strategy …

V 1. z) Bicycle dream

The dream was from the same woman and followed the previous dream.

I am sitting on a racing bike (I never had one in real life) and pedaling with full power. Drizzle claps me uncomfortably in the face, so that I must squint the eyes.

racing bike: power, driven ny one's own strength – obviously unused, unpracticed
rain in the face: to prevail by own strength against adverse circumstances

In front of me I see other, crouched racing cyclists in yellow, tight-fitting suits, who are also racing at full speed over the rain-soaked asphalt. I belong to the group and try not to lose the connection. Like crazy, we whiz past cars, through traffic lights, white lines of the road. Suddenly I miss the group, have lost sight of them. Where are they?

group: apparently the community is being sought – as in the house dream.
It seems to be about a contradiction between conformity and belonging to the community on the one hand and wildness, impudence, maladjustment and belonging to the fringe group community on the other. Is there an underlying fear of rejection and loneliness in disobedience? The oldest layer seems to be the feeling of "I am not seen as I am," which certainly includes a "I am not allowed to be as I am."

The next moment I'm sitting in a hallway on a wooden bench against the wall, the racing bike to my right.

slowed down – being with the force (bicycle) in the bureaucracy/public
the bicycle stands on the right, i.e. on the side that symbolizes the future – hope for more power in the future

A yellowish lamp shines down on me from the ceiling. The hallway bears some resemblance to the teacher's lounge before, but it could also be a youth hostel or hospital. Several yellow doors branch off into other rooms that I can't see; fleetingly, I perceive people and voices from the rooms.
Looking down at my legs, I see a large hole in my left knee. I turn my leg and look with horror and disgust at the deep wound, red, wet flesh as deep as I look, but no

pain. I press the edges of the wound together, it smacks a bit, but somehow the spots don't want to overlap properly. No matter how much I press on it, I can't close the hole. Now a transparent, yellow liquid is leaking out and running down the leg into the sock.

In bureaucracy, the power (leg) is destroyed. The knee belongs to the 10th house in astrology, which represents the public. The public's demands on the woman are destroying her strength and she doesn't know how to heal it ….

I look up and see a white poster on the opposite wall. There is written in sharpie an instruction in several steps what to do to get back to the racing bike group. I can't read the poster properly, it's blurry.

there is hope to get back to the force – but also fear to use this possibility (can't read the writing properly)

I understand that the group leader needs to be called, that he knows the location and will pick one up. Several numbers are listed there but somehow I don't manage to enter them into my cell phone.
- The alarm clock rings. -

and again the way to power leads through the "area" of an authority (group leader) … at least that's how it seems to the woman
not being able to enter the numbers: not being able (or allowed?) to make contact

V 2. Dream diary

With the help of a dream diary one has the possibility to find motive frequencies and motive links: Which motif repeats? In what way does it change?

In the dreams of mine mentioned in the previous chapter, for example, the repression of aggression is a theme that recurs. In the four dreams of the woman, the conflict between conformity and self-assertion is the basic theme.

V 3. Dream journeys

In dream journeys exactly the same symbolism is found as in night dreams. However, dream journeys have the great advantage that one is conscious in them and can therefore ask questions, explore things specifically and make changes in one's own inner imagery.

V 3. a) Opening Scene

The opening scene of a dream journey usually shows what is the outermost shell of the topic in question, that is, how this topic appears to oneself and to others at first glance. This shell contains the latest developments of this topic – the "status quo".

If the dream journey begins in a house, it is about one's own body (=house) or about the togetherness of the people who live together in this house. It is also about structures, about an outer form. The condition of the house says something about the character of these structures. A cozy house indicates well-being, a ruin indicates lost struggles.

If the dream journey begins on a meadow, it is about life force, which is little structured (grass). A forest is already clearly more strongly individualized life force than a meadow (few trees instead of much grass). Pastures are used life force; fields are cultivated life force; parks are cultural life force and so on.

If the dream journey begins in a desert, there is lack of life force; the same applies to a mountain range, with the addition of obstacles.

If the dream journey begins in outer space, it is either about a superordinate, possibly spiritual theme, or about a very basic loneliness.

V 3. b) Path

Paths often appear on dream journeys. By the kind of the picture of this way one can recognize the quality of the way to the topic of the dream journey.

> wide path: one is used to it and has walked it many times
> narrow path: one has walked it only rarely
> meadow: one does not know the path yet, there is no path
> mountain: it is difficult

river: one has to trust it
one flies as a bird: one can walk the path with overview
ravine: one is forced to take a certain path
cave: it leads through a completely inaccessible area on only one way
a dragon blocks one's way: one fears what one might find
a great fire: one is afraid of the power in the place
etc.

V 3. c) Center

In many dream journeys, one wants to get to the essential, which in many cases is a center. Such a center can be marked in various ways: crossroads, temple, lake, lonely mountain, sun, sphere, gold, gold sphere, king, throne, world tree, pyramid, burial mound, city, temple, etc.

V 3. d) Encounters

On dream journeys one encounters many images, most of which are quite easy to interpret:

crossing a river: coming into a new area
encountering a being in the center: possibly one's own soul
encountering a distinctive animal: possibly one's own power animal
encountering a striking plant: possibly one's own power plant
encountering a striking stone: possibly one's own power stone

Everything you encounter is in some way a part of yourself. Therefore, it is always useful to address the being in question. You can simply greet it and ask it if it might show or tell you something.
Directions also have a meaning:

If something moves from left to right, it is going into the future.
When something moves from right to left, it goes into the past.
When something moves from the back to the front (toward you), it is seeking contact.
When something moves from the front to the back (away from you), it

flees.

When something moves from above towards one's own level, it brings power from consciousness.

When something moves upward from one's own level, it strives for realization of the whole.

When something moves up from below to one's own level, it brings life force (kundalini).

When something moves downward from one's own level, it is hiding something or seeking something hidden.

V 3. e) The "golden thread"

If you are stuck, you can wish for a golden ball of wool, knot the end of the wool around your left wrist, and then throw the ball of wool in the air with the words "To the essentials!" Then you follow this "golden thread".

V 3. f) A question for clarification

If you don't understand a picture, you can ask yourself a question about it: "How could the picture be different?" This question makes one's view on the picture clearer.

Why do I see a city and not a meadow? – It is about culture and civilization and not about nature.

Why does the bird fly to the right and not to the left? – Because it points to the future.

Why do I meet a horse and not a lion? – Because it is about community and not about strength.

etc.

V 4.   Visions

The difference between a dream journey and a vision is not very great in content, but quite clear in experience:

> In a dream journey one sees inner images – usually with closed eyes. These images are clearly recognizable as inner images.

> In a vision, the inner image overlaps with the outer image – so one sees the inner image as if it were a part of the real outer world. This can be very impressive, but it requires the person to still be able to distinguish the inner images from the outer images – otherwise these visions would have to be called "hallucination" or "psychosis". One should never lose the clear recognition of the external reality.

V 4. a)   Future

When I was 12 years old, I once stood in front of the mirror and combed my hair. Suddenly a man looked at me out of the mirror. I was quite taken aback. I liked the man, but I was thinking "I will never look like that man." Funnily enough, this event was quite unspectacular and somehow "quite normal".

About six years later, while combing my hair, I stood in front of that same mirror again and suddenly realized that I had seen six years ago exactly how I now looked like.

Some visions (and also some inner images) may also show the future.

V 4. b)   Cuckoo flower

When I was about 22 years old, I once saw a cuckoo flower blooming in a clearing in the woods. For some reason it touched me very much. So I squatted down next to the flower, held my hand next to it and told it how beautiful I thought it was and that I was glad it was there.

All of a sudden I saw a lot of flowers in front of me – colorful, in the brightest colors, in a variety of shapes that changed constantly.

This image overlapped the external perception, but in such a way that I saw two images at the same time, so to speak. I could direct which image (flowers or surroundings) I wanted to see more clearly.

For about a year I only had to think of this cuckoo flower to recall these flower visions.

V 4. c) Laurel Elf

I went to the Canary Island of La Palma with a friend several years ago. On my birthday we hiked through the valley where the last laurel forest on earth is located. Since my friend could not run well uphill, she was exhausted quite soon and has sat down on a rock at the wayside – at the place we have been about 30m above the valley bottom.

As I stood there looking down into the valley and thinking that these laurel forests had once been very widespread, I had the idea of calling the laurel forest elf. I had hardly had this thought when I already saw him – he was standing down in the valley and was so huge that we were at eye level. He didn't seem like a lovely flower spirit either, but was stocky and robust and a bit restrained, though at the same time, well, I can best describe it as "life friendly".

I greeted him and asked him if he could give my friend some strength to keep walking. He nodded, glanced briefly at her, and then continued up the valley.

My perception was like a dream journey with open eyes, where the inner and outer images overlay each other. In contrast to the "cuckoo flower visions", however, both parts resulted in a unified picture, in which, however, both parts could be clearly distinguished – the real landscape was painted, so to speak, with strong oil colors, but the elf was drawn in a semi-transparent way as with colored pencils.

My friend clearly felt the "blessing" of the laurel elf (she did not know that I had just seen it) and actually felt fit again, and instead of turning back we were able to walk up the valley for another half hour.

V 4. d) Pan

Visions do not always have to be visual, they can also be auditory. Many years ago, together with a friend, I once called upon the Greek god Pan in the forest.

Thereupon Pan played briefly in the forest on his flute – there were not many notes, but my hair stood on end because the tones were so intense.

V 4. e) Eagle and snake

Some time later, in the same clearing in the forest, I practiced runes (posture and chanting) – including the rune "Tyr". When I finished and was about to leave, an eagle swooped down from the sky, landed on the ground a few steps in front of me, turned into a snake and crawled away into the brush.

I was thunderstruck … But then I noticed that there were neither eagles nor snakes in the region where I was. So it must have been a vision – and eagles can't turn into snakes either … But if there had been no contradiction in what I had seen, I would not have known that this had been a vision.

As with all Indo-Germanic god fathers (Zeus, Jupiter, Dagda, Shiun etc.) the soul bird of the former Germanic sungod-fathergod Tyr is an eagle. On his afterlife journey the father of the gods turns into a snake, as is reported about Zeus and Tyr among others – but I didn't know all that at that time. So obviously my using the rune "Tyr" had caused a vision of the evening-transformation of Tyr – you could also simply say, that I called Tyr and that he answered my call …

This is the dangerous kind of vision – for I might not have been able to recognize it as a vision if my mind had not spotted the contradicition, i.e. the impossibilities in my perception.

In the sweat lodge ceremony (which I did not know at that time) snake and eagle face each other: instinct and will, the contemplation of the small and the perception of the great. The Mexican city of Tenochtitlan, which was one of the largest cities in the world around 1500 AD, was founded on a vision of an eagle perched on a cactus with a snake in its talons.

The European eagle/snake statues usually depict a fight between these two animals, which is more often associated with a dispute between will and instincts.

V 5. Painting

With the help of the Ba-Gua one can interpret any painting – one gets as an answer the state of the person when painting this painting or even any simple line drawing ("scribble").

Therefore, these line drawings and their interpretations can also be used to recognize a person's state of mind: You let him scribble a few strokes and then look at them.

V 5. a) Line drawing 1

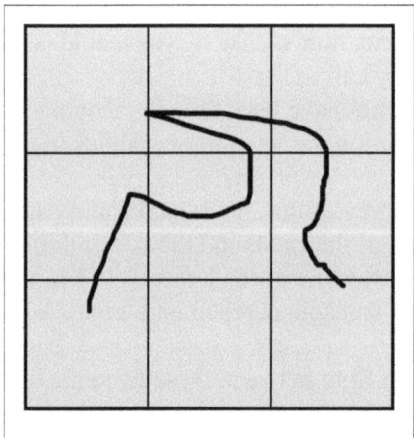

In a line drawing, you have a person draw one or more lines on a piece of paper. In the drawing on the left, the person started on the left.

For the interpretation the picture is divided into 3·3 fields.

The impulse started at a low energy level in the past (bottom left) – the person probably wants to change an unpleasant situation.

He rises with momentum to the middle level, but then bends sharply to the lower right: His momentum, his effort does not last long.

From the middle field, that is, out of himself, he turns to the upper left (high energy in the past): he hopes for help from outside from a supporter – he wants to do something he cannot achieve alone.

After this request for help, he strives upward to his ideal on the right, but then trundles downward (low energy) on the future side (right): his impulse to improve his situation with outside help has failed …

V 5. b) Line drawing 2

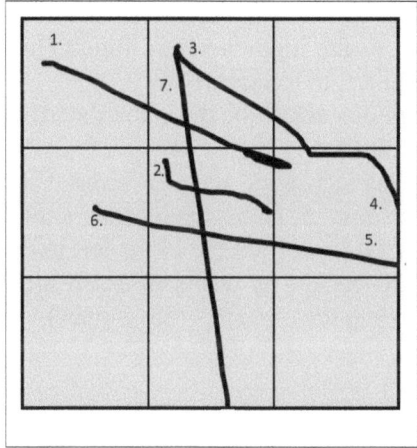

The strokes have been painted almost furiously – between point 4. and 5. they have been painted even over the edge of the paper and also the line that starts at point 7. has been painted over the sheet at the bottom.

The line that starts at 1. wants to get help from the field on the upper left and anchor itself in the middle – a hook has been painted there.

The line that begins at point 2. repeats this movement with much less verve and exclusively in the central field, i.e. within the ego.

The next stroke begins at point 3. and is like an angry repetition of the two previous strokes – but here, too, help is no longer asked for in the upper left field. The stroke crashes, goes angrily beyond the edge of the paper, and then shoots back from point 5. to the left to point 6.: a massive, angry, accusatory regression – the subject is convinced that he is entitled to something specific from the top left or middle left field. Top left is a patron or the like; center left is the family of origin – presumably the mother.

Finally, a fourth stroke starts at the same place as the third stroke (7.) and shoots steeply down within the middle column (present, I) – the ultimate crash. Resignation and depression …

V 5. c) Line drawing 3

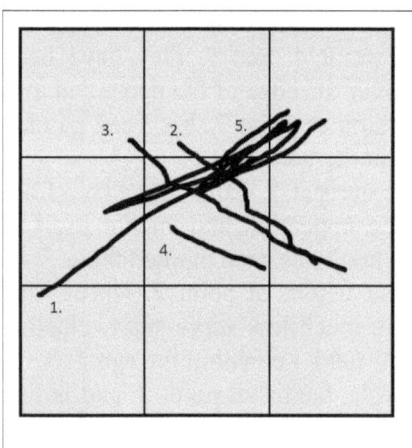

Here someone wants to go from the low-energetic past to the high-energetic future (line 1. from bottom left to top right).

But there are obstacles: the three lines starting at point 2., 3. and 4.

But the subject does not let himself be intimidated: at point 5. he begins to draw a total of five connected lines from the lower left to the upper right and back – he wants to assert himself and overcome the obstacles (cross lines).

V 5. d) Picture

The same procedure can be applied to classical paintings – such as the painting "Starry Night" by van Gogh.

At the top right (target) is the moon as the most striking element in the painting – it was the motivation for painting.

Below is a city on the low level – van Gogh wanted to go beyond this level.

On the left, a thuja or something similar towers darkly – the striving for a higher level of energy, which has not led to much in the past, as it remains dark. The dark tree is a blockade. Thus, the moon is the symbol of the dream of reaching a goal that has not been reached in the past.

Mountains rise from the lower left to the center right – a dark row of mountains below, a lighter row of mountains above. The line rising to the right is the movement of hope for better times – this line leads from low energy in the past to high energy in the future: success – but up to now only a success in dreams (moon). The light above the dark has the same meaning.

From the upper left, a vortex enters the center, but then runs out to the center right. This is hope for help from outside – perhaps also the hope for the approval of a woman for a relationship, because the line ends on the right in the middle, where the self-founded family is located. There on the far right in the center the contrast of dark and light is also strongest – the essence of the dramatics of the feelings underlying this picture.

V 6.   Archaeology

In archaeology one sometimes finds pictures - without any explanation … Therefore, the correct interpretation of pictures is also important in archaeology.

V 6. a)   Cave painting

In the cave paintings, which are between 45,000 and 14,000 years old, more than 95% are animals.

In a first step, one can check whether the animals depicted correspond in frequency to the animals in the environment of the people of that time – then the paintings would be nothing more than a "photograph", so to speak. However, this is not the case.

Then one can check whether the stomach has guided the hand of the artist – whether the proportions of the depicted animals correspond to the preserved food remains (mainly bones). This is also not the case.

So the animals must represent characteristics that were important to the people of that time. So one can check, for example, where in the caves the individual animal species are found. Since they are not evenly distributed, one can infer their symbolic character from their preference for certain places (entrance, passage, all the way inside, small side chambers, etc.).

One can also check which motifs often appear together and which never appear next to each other. From this a "sociogram" of the motives can be formed.

This procedure is not much different from the interpretation of a dream diary …

V 6. b)   Göbekli Tepe

Also in the early Neolithic we have only pictures and statuettes, but no explanations – writing was invented only in the early kingdoms.

Here, essentially the same questions as before can be asked, since the first temples in the early Neolithic (Göbekli Tepe, Nevali Cori, etc.) correspond in their symbolism to the caves of the Paleolithic.

> What occurs how often?
> What occurs how often together with another motif?
> What is always in a certain place of the temple?

What is always found, for example, on the front of the columns?
What is always located in a certain direction?
Which motifs are also known from cave paintings?
Which motifs are also known from later religions?

These questions can also be applied analogously to the interpretation of the inner images of people.

V 7. Graphology

Graphology is the reading of the character of a person from his style of writing.

- dense writing = concentration, narrowness, possibly fear
- wide, loose writing = agility, jumpiness, possibly lack of concentration
- high ascenders (for "t", "d", "b", etc.) = want to reach high
- long descenders (at "p", "q", "g" etc.) = search for roots (hold)
- inclined upwards to the right = optimism
- inclined upwards to the left = despondency
- quite straight = strictly adheres to rules
- many squiggles = obsessive
- i-dots etc. far away from the letter = tattered, possibly unreliable
  etc.

Here we find the same principles as in Ba-Gua.

V 8. Facial expressions

The facial expression is a fixed system of movements of the facial muscles, which are instinctively understood and cannot be precisely described by most people. The direction of the corners of the mouth is fairly well known, but e.g. the smile lines in the outer corners of the eyes are less so.

V 9. Gestures

The manner of movement says as much as facial expressions: fast, slow, despondent, uncertain, with sudden changes of direction, vehement, reckless, and so on. This is also a form of an image.

V 10. Speech melody

The same applies to the speech melody. Is it monotonous? Does it always rise? Is it regular, melodic, choppy, busy, breathy, rough, unpredictable? Do gaps appear between words? Does the voice sometimes fail? Is it busy, melodious, with natural vibrato, with overtones, firm, secure, hard?

The voice creates a sound image independent of the specific words, which says a lot about the person in question.

V 11. Self-similarity

"Self-similarity" means that all parts of an organic system have the same properties and structures – all parts of a system have the same astrological chart ...

This self-similarity is found in people in the palm lines, in the foot reflex zones, in the iris diagnosis, the image of the body on the face (forehead = head; brows = arms; nose = body; nostrils = genitals; mouth = anus; upper jaw = thigh; jaw joint = knee; lower jaw = lower leg; chin = feet), the image of the body on the ear, and so on.

Ultimately, the quality of the body system can be found in every part of the body, if one has studied that part of the body thoroughly enough. The same quality can be found everywhere in the body – and also an image of the whole body in the part.

V 12.   Diseases

Diseases are also images. They begin with a mental/emotional disorder which, if not corrected, becomes a physical disorder.

V 12. a)   Elbow pain

The arm is the part of the body with which one acts. The upper arm gives the general direction to the surrounding space, the forearm coordinates on the spot and the hand grasps and releases. Thus, the upper arm is the public, the forearm is the family, and the hand is the relationship.

Pain in the elbow thus indicates that the person cannot bring public and family together – presumably he is doing something that he does not want to be generally known.

V 12. b)   Breast cancer

Cancer is a disease in which cells multiply excessively and without function – cancer is therefore a Jupiter disease. It lacks the realization of the actual goals, which leads to a functionless multiplication.

The organ in which the cancer forms shows in which area one's goals could not be achieved. In the case of breast cancer, these are closeness, security and nutrition.

V 12. c)   Exhaustion

A woman sought advice from me because of a prolonged state of exhaustion. Upon closer questioning, it turns out that the exhaustion is possibly due to an allergy and that this allergy exists especially against the pollen of birches, willows and poplars, whereby the allergic rash occurs mainly on the abdomen below the navel and is often associated with headaches.

Since allergy is a disorder of the body's immune system based on the fact that

a) the body erroneously classifies certain substances (in this case pollen) as threatening and defends itself against them,

84

b) such a reaction occurs most often when the body is already highly irritated by foreign substances (chemicals in food, water and air), and

c) the body's defense system is also irritated by psychological stress,

it can be assumed that the person in question is repressing aggression, is therefore in a state of subliminal aggression, and that this aggression has sought a substitute opponent, in this case the pollen. The exhaustion of this woman is therefore primarily due to her repression of aggression and secondarily due to the stress on the body caused by the allergy.

The question now arises why the allergy is directed precisely against the pollen of the birch, the willow and the poplar. First of all, it is noticeable that the pollen is the male seed, i.e. the equivalent of the human male sperm, which suggests a sexual theme associated with aggression repression. So why is the allergy directed precisely against the pollen of these three trees and not against that of rose, buttercup and apple?

The special thing about the birch is that, on the one hand, it is a pioneer plant and almost always the first to settle in clearings and windthrows, and on the other hand, it transports a very large amount of water in its wood – when you cut down a birch, sap still runs out of the rootstock for several hours.

The willow is a water-loving tree and is extremely capable of regeneration.

The poplar is able to transport water in its trunk to very high altitudes.

All three trees are botanically close relatives and are associated with water. So these trees symbolize the transport of water in the body and the life force associated with that water.

Now, taking together the transport of water to great heights and the life force associated with it, as well as repressed sexuality and aggression, there is an association with the sushumna, the channel in which the life force rises up the spine as tummo fire (kundalini). Thus, one could conjecture that the woman in question has a blockage in the sushumna that blocks sexuality and aggression, which is confirmed by the fact that the allergic rash is located in the hara area, where one should also expect the blockage of the sushumna if the life force has been caused by a blockage of sexuality, which is located in the root chakra.

The headache that occurs together with the allergy points to the Hara/ Third Eye polarity, where the Hara is the place of energy deficiency and the Third Eye is the area of energy congestion. So we can assume that the woman in question is trying to get along in the world by pleasing everyone (Third Eye energy congestion), and that she is easily upset (Hara energy deficiency) – the constitution of a victim.

Now there is a stone that has exactly the qualities of these trees – fire opal. It is formed in hot geysers, that is, in a place where hot water rises. In this hot rising water, silica and iron oxide is dissolved, which then combines in the deposits around the geyser, first to a gel and then to a reddish stone. This stone acts very quickly and violently and makes cheerful, impulsive and enthusiastic and also kindles repressed sexual fire (hot liquids occur in the process) and sometimes leads to nosebleeds (blood = hot liquid; nose corresponds to genitals) or a violently running sniffling nose (hot liquid again).

Therefore, one could put a fire opal on the allergic rash of the woman in question once and see if this is enough to get the pent-up fire going again. The analogy between the rising tummo fire, the rising sperm, the pollen of the trees, the rising water in the trees and the rising hot water in the geyser as well as the marsic symbolism of the iron in the fire opal is the basis for this attempt.

Sometimes, when the blockage is too strong, instead of a rising of the life force, one reacts with a nosebleed – a hot, ferruginous, red liquid full of life force rises up and seeks a way out. The nosebleed in this case is obviously a detour of the life force, the stimulation of which cannot be prevented by the body and the psyche, but can at least be "diverted" into the symbolic equivalent of the genitals in the face. In this case, the woman in question would obviously not yet be ready to give up the blockage of her sexuality quickly.

V 13.   Epidemics

In a plague, a great many people are affected by the same disease. Here, too, one may look to see what the psychic cause may be – which in this case must be a collective cause.

V 13. a)   Corana virus

The Corona virus attacks the lungs, that is, the rhythmic system of the human being. Breathing needs freedom and expansiveness and unhindered self-expression in order to function – otherwise it becomes tight around the chest and one gets trepidation.

Both the Sars disease (2002) and the much worse Corana virus (2020) originated in China. There, the Communist Party is exerting ever more massive pressure on people's behavior. By the introduction of the social point-system in China a hardly concealed dressage of the behavior of humans is aimed at. This makes the chest tight, hard and depressed – the ideal basis for any form of lung disease.

V 14.   Homeopathy

In homeopathy, one looks at the image of the disease, i.e., more precisely, the image of the condition of a patient – and then looks for a remedy that produces exactly this image in a healthy person.

This can be seen as an analogy spell – the remedy that evokes a certain image cures itself in a sick person.

Recognizing these images requires the same form of creativity, of "thinking differently" as in interpreting dreams – here, too, the "language of the moon" is used.

V 15. Symbols

Symbols are, so to speak, single words of the picture language. There are some words which are more or less universal because of their age and simplicity – but one should always look for the context in which a motif appears and whether it can really have the traditional meaning there.

The following are only four examples of ancient and important symbols.

V 15. a) Sun

The sun is the most widespread symbol of the soul – there is nothing that would attract the eye more and that would be more conspicuous.

The sun also gives orientation, as one can tell the points of the compass by its position in the sky. This has resulted in the sun symbol, which consists of a circle and a cross in it: horizon, four cardinal points and center.

From this motif was derived the four-faced sun god, who rules all four directions, that is, the whole earth. This gave rise to the motif of the sun as a four-spoked wheel. By bending the four spokes and omitting the "rim" of the wheel, the swastika was created – the wheel of fire whirling along the sky.

From the cycle symbolism of the "3" has resulted the sun disk with three legs as a celestial wanderer – the triskelis.

V 15. b) Serpent

The dead lie in the earth – therefore it was natural to represent the dead as snakes, because snakes live on and in the earth and in crevices.

By combining the snake with the soul bird and the burial fire, they became fire-breathing, winged dragons.

Since the ancestors can send a blessing to their descendants from the underworld, this blessing was also represented as a snake – from this also the Kundalini snake originates.

The path to the underworld was also seen as a snake. The path of the sun from the western horizon under the earth to the eastern horizon became a giant snake. This giant serpent was later reinterpreted as the rain-robbing serpent, which robs the rain in summer and wages an endless cyclic battle with the sky god. This is the origin of the battle of the sky eagle against the earth serpent.

V 15. c) Burial Mound

The first hut, 1.7 million years ago, was the first interior space, the first shelter, experienced by the people of that time. It has been associated, obviously, with the womb of the mother.

When with the beginning of the ice age 600,000 years ago the heating of these huts with hot stones was added, the sweat hut developed, which was understood as the belly of the large mother.

Since the arrival in the afterlife was imagined as a rebirth, it was obvious to build a hut or simply a pile of brushwood over graves, which represented the belly of the earth that was pregnant with the dead.

The sweat lodges became the first temples at the beginning of the Neolithic period, 12,000 years ago, which were half-stone sweat lodges. The sticks, from which the frame of the sweat lodge had been built, were replaced by stone pillars – both of which represented the ancestors.

About 8000 years ago, the brushwood mounds became the tumuli (burial mounds) built of stones and earth.

The menhir complexes have resulted from the first temples by the reduction to the ancestor stone pillars.

V 15. d) Totem pole

The totem pole in the Paleolithic period was initially a simple staff with a bird on it - the symbol of the soul bird that could be experienced, for example, by astral travel during a near-death.

In the late Paleolithic, i.e., for about 50,000 years, this bird staff became larger and more complex and grew into a totem pole, but in essence it always remained "a man with his soul bird."

V 16. Omen

An omen is an event that has a meaning in the context in which it takes place. An omen is, so to speak, an "event-picture" and can therefore be interpreted like all other images – omens also speak the "language of the moon".

V 16. a) Flight of birds

Since the ancestors are, on the one hand, the "wise and helpful beings" and, on the other hand, have the form of soul-birds, one has tried worldwide to interpret the flight of the birds as a hint of the ancestors to the questions which their descendants have had.

V 16. b) Three arrows

I have been friends with a couple who are both sculptors. I would have liked to have had closer contact with the woman.

One day I was standing by a work of art that they had made together. Then the question came up in me what would actually happen if I would simply do what I felt like doing and not constantly take their relationship into consideration.

Immediately after I became aware of this possibility of action and this question, I felt the urge to go to the ditch that ran 10m away from the artwork. When I looked down the 4m into this ditch, through which a brook from the forest flowed down into the valley, I saw three arrows stuck in the ground down by the brook.

Then I went down into the ditch and took a closer look at these arrows. On the side of the brook, which lay to the work of art, two equal arrows stuck side by side in the earth; on the other side a different-looking arrow stuck in the earth, whose point was missing and whose notch was half broken off.

The interpretation was not difficult: the man was Sagittarius by the sign of the zodiac, i.e. he symbolically gave me the answer with the arrows – so the omen was possibly influenced by the man's point of view.

Two same arrows are a pair – on the artwork side of the stream – the couple. The third arrow is separated from this pair by the brook. It is also "neutered" by the broken-off notch and missing tip.

This didn't look like much was going to happen between me and the woman ….

V 17.   Family constellations

In a family constellation, as in facial expressions, gestures and homeopathy, there is an "action-picture". This image is the family tradition, that is, a certain pattern of behavior that has developed over time and is passed on from parents to children. Through family constellations this picture may become clearer – and above all may be also changed.

V 18.   Crop circles

Crop circles are obviously pictures – but not on paper or on canvas, but in grain fields.

The crop circles are most probably not created by humans. When one enters a newly created crop circle, it feels like a transfer of power, like in a powerful ritual, like in an effective consecration or in a similar processes. This suggests a telekinetic origin of the crop circles.

In addition it fits among other things also that the grain stalks were often bent down at the knots of the stalks – which is physically impossible, since the stalks would break thereby.

But from whom originates this nevertheless very powerful and complex telekinesis goes? From the collective subconsciousness of the people? Or is it Gaia, that is the earth as a whole?

The grain elf as the originator is rather unlikely, because why should he do that? There the collective subconsciousness of humans or Gaia are more probable – both could have a motivation. However, not all the crop circles can be "read" as a clear message so far.

A encompassing consideration of crop circles and their symbolism may be found in my book „Crop Dircles for Beginners".

V 18. a)   Polarity

The structure of some crop circles is easy to understand. One of these "understandable crop circles" consists in the center of a large ring, in which the energy pulsates.

This ring is divided by a straight line into two equal halves. At the two places where this straight line ends at the ring, there is a small circle outside the large ring each – one of them is a circular surface which is widening and feels like a mountain; the other of them is a circular ring which is contracting and feels like a cave.

These two outer circles are the two poles that make the energy flow and pulsate in the large central ring.

Without the large ring, that is, just the two outer circles and the straight line, we get the astrological symbol for the opposition. One can understand the large ring in this context as the zodiac, in which this astrological opposotion-aspect is situated.

This crop circle corresponds in its structure to what Rudolf Steiner called "three-structure".

V 18. b)   Symbols

Some crop circles also represent well-known symbols and graphics like the mathematical Mandelbrot set, the mathematical Julia set or the three uppermost Sephiroth of the Kabbalistic Tree of Life.

V 19. Objects

Objects are also images in the sense of the "language of the moon". However, this is not too often of greater importance. However, when one uses an object in magic or otherwise gives it great significance, for example, as a symbol, the message of its image becomes important.

There is an order in which the properties of this object are important:

1. what the object represents, e.g., a ring in the shape of a snake or a Eucharistic chalice or a statue of Buddha is most important;

2. the shape of the object, i.e. a closed or open snake ring, a slim or wide Eucharist chalice, the posture of the Buddha statue, etc.;

3. the symbols and the like attached, e.g. a gemstone in the head of the ring-snake, a cross on the chalice, or the demon Maya in front of the Buddha statue;

4. the material from which the object was made, e.g. gold (sun), silver (moon) or copper (Venus);

5. the quality (craftsmanship) in which the object was made, is least improtant.

Therefore, it is useful to know the history of the object, i.e. the symbolism of the snakes or the chalice, or the history and teachings of Buddha. This is what will ultimately be revealed by the object if it is given a central position in any context.

The snake will always be a symbol of the life force, kundalini, ancestors, the after-life path, etc. – no matter what associations are made with this snake.

When the ring is closed, the life force will be trapped – at best it will be an image of the sleeping Kundalini, at worst it will be an image of the trapped life force and thus the shadow of the life force. When the ring is open, the life force is free and the Kundalini is able to rise.

If the ring-snake wears a ruby on its head, it will be fiery; if it wears a diamond on its head, it will be single-minded; if it wears an apache tear on its head, it will be very vehement; if it wears a fire opal on its head, it will act mainly on the kundalini, etc.

The material of which the object is made is, so to speak, the "color" of the "image": gold represents the sun, the heart chakra, the soul and the radiance; silver represents the life force, the six outer chakras and the flow; iron represents power, strength, deeds and action, etc. The material shows in which form or in which area the object has a preferential effect.

The quality of workmanship has little significance – a particularly carefully crafted object is more impressive and therefore more suitable for use in collective rituals and the like than one that is only crudely formed, but even a plain voodoo doll can work well.

Another aspect of the image of objects is the idea that one inwardly associates with that object. However, these unconscious ideas or intentional imaginations will not prevail against the form of the object – a sword is simply an unsuitable symbol for love and a Buddha statue is not suitable for a spell spoken by hatred.

V 20. Oracles

In oracles pictures or symbols are used, which in their totality represent the world and are therefore a mirror image of the world, so that one can recognize the state of the world on the basis of the pictures or symbols selected "by meaningful coincidence".

These pictures or symbols are already defined in their meaning in the traditional systems from the beginning and are therefore fixed. Only in oracle systems, which are based on objects, which have a meaning only for the user, these pictures and/or symbols are individual (e.g. the tooth of a predator, by which one was hurt once; a crystal, which one found during a ritual etc.).

V 21. Names

Names can be images, if they describe the signified. The simplest form of such a name are designations like "cuckoo", which derive from the call of the animal concerned.

However, there are also names that have a larger story behind them. A good example of this is the name of the Aztec god Tezcatlipoca, which means "smoking-mirror."

Tezcatlipoca is a shaman god and god of war – similar to the Germanic Odin. Just as the bear is the animal of Odin, the jaguar is the animal of Tezcatlipoca – the large predator is the companion of shamans worldwide.

As a shaman god, Tezcatlipoca can also be clairvoyant, i.e. perceive the life force. Popular tools for learning clairvoyance are the crystal ball and the mirror – they are the canvas onto which one can project inner images. The image that appears in the crystal ball or on the mirror is a "localized vision", so to speak – the vision is limited to the crystal ball or to the mirror.

The smoke in general has the symbolism of life force and breath among the Indians – similar to the ideas of the Egyptians, who for this reason called the incense "senetjer", i.e. "that which makes divine". Because of this idea, the Indians use a pipe in rituals – they incense with tobacco in this way. The pipe bowl represents what the Indian connects to when smoking, and the pipe stem (world tree, middle pillar, umbilical cord) is the connection to what the pipe bowl represents (god, ghost, animal).

So a "smoking mirror" is a mirror in which the life force appears. In the West, this is usually referred to as milky white mist that appears in the crystal ball or mirror.

So the god Tezcatlipoca is the god who can see the life force and who helps the shamans to see the life force as well.

V 22. Horoscope

A horoscope is a "graphic image" that represents the quality of a moment. All things that become independent at a certain moment, i.e. a person at his birth, a company at its foundation, etc., retain this quality as long as they exist.

A horoscope is constructed like a play, which is an "action-picture":

ascendant:	stage set
planets:	actora
zodiac signs:	roles of the actors
houses:	places on stage (actors' areas of action).
aspects:	script
center of the horoscope:	director (conscious ego)
above the horoscope:	script writer (soul)

V 23. Numbers and Angles

There are some numbers and their corresponding angles that have a general meaning (for more details see my book "Number symbolism for Beginners").

These numbers are:

1, 0°, 360°:	identity, concentration, "marrige"
2, 180° (1/2 of a circle):	complemantary opposition, Yin and Yang, day and night, eternal change
3, 120° (1/3 of a circle):	evolution, unfolding, development, "friendship"
4, 90° (1/4 of a circle):	segregation, stability, form
5, 150° (5/12 of a circle):	solving and combining, modifying
6, 60° (1/6 of a circle):	group of similar items, "acquaintance"
12, 30° (1/12 of a circle):	taking the next step, "chance meeting"
12 (one whole circle):	organic form

V 24.   Dream journey examples

The two areas where understanding the "language of the moon" is most important, or where this language is most often used, are the interpretation of dreams and the interpretation of dream journeys.

The following two dream journeys are two examples of a journey to one's own center, that is, to one's own soul. In these dream journeys I accompanied the persons concerned and we talked to each other during the dream journey. I am not in the dream journey, i.e. in the images that the person sees – I am sitting next to them on the outside, but I still see a large part of the images myself.

V 24. a)   Dream journey to one's own center 1

In her imagination the woman steps through the center symbol (a hexagram with the sun in the center). She opens a door on which the symbol is located and sees a hilly landscape with a lot of grass, avenues with trees, everything is strong and green, the sun is shining.

grass: barely organized life force
alley: The path to the center is obviously clear and has been walked on many times. Here the life force has already organized itself into trees standing in rows.
strong and green: vitality
sun: symbol of the middle

Harry: "Is there something that attracts you?"
The woman has no particular focus and just enjoys the view of the landscape.

enjoyment: being at peace with yourself

Harry: "Find a stick and determine which point should be the top. Put it on the ground and let it spin. Then have it point to the center in the vision."
Woman: "It points forward away from me."

forward: directly toward the target

Harry: "Do you want to go there?"
Woman: "Yes."

Harry: "What's there?"
Woman: "A house made of red brick, rather small, a hut with big windows."

house: place of residence, civilization
big windows: open to the world

Harry: "Do you want to go in?"
Woman: "Yes."
Harry: "What do you see there?"
  Woman: "Not much, it's all dark downstairs. I'll go up the stairs – it's all light there."

lower floor: belly – is there a problem there? Something unconscious?
upper floor: head – conscious views ... adjustment?

Harry: "What do you see?"
Woman: "Window with light coming in, an empty room, an attic, no furniture."

empty attic: empty head? What is missing here?
window: contact with the outside world

Harry: "Take a handful of light downstairs and see what's downstairs."
  Woman: "The darkness was threatening, now it's a cozy living room with couch, book nook, fireplace ..."

Why was the room dark? Was she not aware that you can be at home in your belly?

  Harry: "Do you like to ask the house what usually happens upstairs in the empty room?"
Woman: "I can't figure it out ..."

Why is the upstairs room empty? Has something been displaced there?

Harry: "Do you like to summon the being who owns the house?"
Woman: "It belongs to an old man."
Harry: "Would you like to describe him?"
  Woman: "He has a very large white beard, is short and stout, has loving and gentle features."

That sounds like wisdom – that wisdom resides in one's body ... an old, male wisdom in the body of a young woman? Why is this a man?

Harry: "Is he trying to tell you something or show you something?"
Woman: "He's showing me his garden, pond and horses."

The old man is obviously close to nature and represents an organic wisdom.

Harry: "Does one horse in particular appeal to you?"
Woman: "A brown horse, light brown-beige, I have already seen it when I went to the house."
Harry: "Does the horse want to tell you or show you something?"
Woman: "I want to go for a ride with him."
Harry: "Do you want to do that?"
Woman: "Yes."

Is thus her power animal? Or simply the power of her own body? Since the horse belongs to the old man, and since the pond and garden and horse also belong to the house, it is more likely simply the power of her body.

Harry: "What do you experience?"
Woman: "The feeling of galloping fast ... the landscape changes, big white mountains with snow on top ... I'm riding through a tunnel ..."
Harry: "Is on both sides of the tunnel the same landscape?"
Woman: "The tunnel is black inside ..."
Harry: "For example, did you ride into the tunnel in a meadow and come out in a desert?"
Woman: "No, on both sides is the same ... mountainous, hilly, the same flora and fauna ... it's both similar ..."

Why is there a dark tunnel in the landscape if it leads nowhere else? It leads under big mountains – big mountains are something big, important, a prominent shape, an important feature of the psyche. The mountains are not a border and the tunnel is not a connection, because on both sides is the same. The power leads through this tunnel – is this possibly the vagina of the woman? Then the horse would be among other things also her own sexual power. But the tunnel has two openings – that does not fit to the interpretation as the vagina.

Harry: "Does the horse know something particularly important for you?"
Woman: "I don't know ..."
Harry: "Do you feel like riding back to the house?"

Woman: "Not really."

Does the woman want to preserve in herself the freedom and power of the horse?

Harry: "Do you feel like asking if the old man might come to you?"
Woman: "Yes."
Harry: "Has he come to you?"
Woman: "Yes, we are sitting together by the lake."

They are both sitting by the pond/lake at the old man's house. He seems to be leading the woman.

Harry: "Would you like to ask him who he is?"
Woman: "Yes – he says he is the Now."

The old man seems to be some kind of Taoist – being in the Here and Now, nature-bound, he knows the power (horse) and apparently more – something that is in the pond …

Harry: "Would you like to tell him that you are looking for your center? – Can he tell you how to get there?"
Woman: "Yes ... he says: recognize the beauty. He suggests that I swim through lake at which we are sitting."

Beauty is the harmony of all parts of a whole. The basis of this harmony is the self-similarity of all parts of this whole. Beauty appears when all parts are as they really are, because then the self-similarity of all parts to each other becomes visible – beauty.
   A lake in a plain could be a symbol of the center – it appears on many dream journeys to the center. A lake is deep water, which consequently could be hiding something.

Harry: "Do you like to do that?"
Woman: "Yes."
Harry: "What are you experiencing?"
Woman: "I love the refreshing temperature of the water, I swim and swim ... there is an island ... birds come to me ... everything is full of life, everything is fertile ... I come to the shore of the island, I stand there, I let the place affect me ..."

Lake, island, refreshment, life, fertility – this place must be close to the center.

Harry: "Do you like to ask the center to show itself to you?"
Woman: "Yes."
Harry: "What are you experiencing?"
Woman: "I shouted the question into the distance ... there came a very large majes-tic bird ... it revealed itself to me ... it is white shining like a swan, but much larger than a swan and also larger than me ... it brings with it a very great stillness and a great peace ... it comes towards me ..."

This sounds like the power animal ... possibly also the mother goddess of swans, since the bird is clearly larger than a swan.

The stillness and peace indicate either the soul or the swan-mother-goddess. Neither of them are typical characteristics of the power animals.

Harry: "What are you experiencing now?"
Woman: "I feel totally touched by this encounter, very comforted ... silence, securi-ty, safety ..."
Harry: "What do you experience?"
Woman: "I'm walking around on the island with the swan ... in the middle of the island is a clearing, there is something very bright, like very a steep hill in the middle, which shines golden-yellow in the sunlight ..."

The way to the center here consists of concentric circles: Plain – lake – island – hill – golden glow.

The concentric, the gold and the glow are all three sure symbols of the center.

Harry: "Do you like to stand in the light?"
Woman: "Yes ... the light is totally warm and energizing ... I start laughing out loud ... I'm catching butterflies and running wild in the area and feeling all playful and bright and alive ... the swan is nearby, but he's lying quietly next to it watching me play ... I found a big glass ball on the hill ..."

The glass ball is once again a step further to the middle – and also again a frequent middle symbol. This symbol originates from the sun – and it appears also in myths and fairy-tales as the golden ball of the princess, who has been originally the beyond-goddess.

The woman is apparently discovering her actual, powerful and playful nature here – butterfly-like ...

Harry: "Would you like to ask her what she is?"
Woman: "Yes ... she does not answer, but I look at glass ball and see a mirror-

image of myself."

    Harry: "Do you have a feeling about it?"

    Woman: "The reflection seems new to me ... I am much more childlike than I thought ... I am surprised ... I can't really recognize myself ..."

The reflection is another indication that the woman has found her center – but apparently doesn't quite know herself yet.

    Harry: "Can you recognize features?"

    Woman: "I wear a red hat or something like that ... otherwise I can't really recognize anything ..."

Is the red hat a sign of power?

    Harry: "May you ask the young face why it appears to you?"
    Woman: "To recognize myself."
    Harry: "Do you recognize yourself?"
    Woman: "No."
    Harry: "May you ask the face what you can do to recognize yourself?"
    Woman: "The face says, 'Become a child again.'"
    Harry: "Do you know how to do that?"
    Woman: "Be in the Now, play ..."
    Harry: "What happens now?"

Here the old man's statement is repeated, embodying the Now. Through the Now, the woman becomes a child again.

    Woman: "The ball has fallen from my hand, it rolls down the hill of light to the swan ... I go down the hill, the swan takes the ball ... we walk through the forest on the island, come to a bog ... that bog is not in the light, but in the shadow, really dark, threatening, gloomy, black, no longer in the sun ..."

Here the woman approaches the problem: it is hidden in the dark – as before in the lower floor in the house.

    Harry: "Do you like to ask the swan about the darkness?"
    Woman: "Yes ... he says nothing, but he shows me to look, to turn my attention to the bog and see ... I observe fist-sized, round, black stones/chunks coming up from the bog and floating in the air ... they are not like stones, but rather alive, but they are not living beings either ..."

The problem comes up from below the darkness: the dark, lower floor of the house, the stones in the bog, and probably the dark tunnel under the big mountain …

Such repetitions of symbols, situations or structures are very typical for the journey to one's own centre.

Harry: "Do you like to ask the stones what they are, why they come?"
Woman: "There comes nothing clear that I could formulate …"
Harry: "May you ask the swan if where you are is enough for you to see yourself?"
Woman: "The swan says nothing, but I understand him wordlessly: I am to feel and understand these black parts … I open my belly and my chest, all the parts fly into me and I see that they are in very great pain, like cramps, like a strong suffering and screaming until I collapse …"

Obviously here an old pain has been repressed that was in the chest and stomach – the lower house floor, the tunnel under the mountain, the black stones in the bog … and the upper floor did not know about it and neither the snow on top of the mountains and the light on the hill …

Harry: "Do you like to ask the swan for help?"
Woman: "Yes … he already helps even without my asking him … I lie on the swan, he goes on walking, he leaves the bog, he goes through the forest …"

The forest is an indication of organized life force.

Harry: "Can the swan or the light tell you if you should do anything else with the stones inside you or if it's good this way?"
Woman: "I am to go to the river and wash them out … wash myself out and thereby wash out the stones … I go to the river, wash myself out and wash out stones … the water is blue, I am right at the source of the river … it gushes there out of the earth … it washes the black color out of the stones … the water turns dark from it … I find my energy back, I can walk again …"

Apparently, the healing consists of the return to the flow (river) – which corresponds to the "Now" of the old man and the face in the sphere.

Harry: "Where are you now?"
Woman: "I'm on the swan, we're in the air, we're flying … we're flying past the old man who's still sitting by the lake … we're just flying on … we have no destination …"
Harry: "Would you like to ask the swan if you've seen enough for today or if there's

anything else he'd like to show you?"
   Woman: "I have seen enough for today."
   Harry: "Then return to the entrance, say thank you and goodbye if you like, and then return through the door."
   Woman: "Yes."
   Harry: "Are you back?"
   Woman: "Yes."

V 24. b)   Dream journey to one's center 2

The Man goes through the door with the center symbol (hexagram with sun in the center).
   Man: "There seems to be fog here ... smoke, mist ..."

What the man sees when he turns to his inner self is fog – he is not used to seeing himself, or is afraid of seeing himself.

Harry: "Is the fog all still, or is it moving somewhere?"
   Man: "Nah, it's so cloudy, so swirling around ..."
   Harry: "Is it all moving from left to right, or is it all swirling in circles?"
   Man: "It's swirling just like that ... so no particular direction."
   Harry: "What color is it?"
   Man: "Gray ... gray-white ..."
   Harry: "Is there anything in any direction that is lighter or darker, quieter or more moving or something ..."
   Man: "Hm ... it's more like a uniform gray ..."
   Harry: "In your mind, do you like to just walk forward a few steps and just see if all stays the same or if something changes?"

The "not seeing anything" is quite pronounced.

Man: "Hm ... well, to be honest, I'm a little afraid that it might go down there ..."

Obviously, the man is afraid of his own inner self.

Harry: "Aha ... then squat down in your imagination and put your hands on the earth – that is, on what you are standing on. Can you feel what that is? Is it earth or cloth or wood or ... whatever?"

Man: "I would say earth."

Harry: "Mhm ... if you feel more closely – is it sandy, is it humus, are there stones in it?"

Man: "Yes, sandy ..."

Harry: "Sandy ..."

Man: "But firm sand ..."

Harry: "Ah yes ... can you dig in it with your hands or is it too firm?"

Man: "No – it's too firm ..."

Harry: "Ah yes ... so almost like sandstone."

Man: "Yeah."

Harry: "Can you see what color it is?"

Man: "Yes – dark brown."

Sand is crushed rock – there has been a great force that has destroyed the original forms. Also the color of the sand has not been able to retain a distinctive character – brown is the mixture of all colors, so no clear standpoint, possibly also a "rotting process".

Harry: "Mhm ... can you just look around, if you notice something somewhere, if there is something lying there or if something looks different?"

Man: "I have the feeling that I'm standing on a mountain somehow – there are some rocks ... there are some ledges at the bottom ... that's why I had the feeling that I could fall down there ... if I just go forward ..."

Harry: "Mhm ... would you like to go to one of these rocks?

Man: "Yes ... but that's only possible in a squat position ... it's all fog over there ..."

Harry: "Oh, there's no fog down there?"

Man: "Nah, there's clear visibility."

Harry: "You can, if you want, ask this fog who it is and why it's actually there."

Man: "The fog?"

Harry: "Yes, address the fog: 'Hello fog – who are you? What are you doing here?'"

Man: "Somehow there's nothing ..."

Harry: "Mhm ..."

It sounds as if the man is afraid to even ask – the fear of his own inner self is quite strong.

The rock is the only solid, striking thing – and the man's fear ...

Man: "Yes, somehow I don't dare to go up there into the fog – it somehow has a very negative effect on me ... it's also dark up there ..."

Harry: "Yes, then just stay down there where you are."

Man: "Mhm."
Harry: "You could also just try calling a wind to clear the fog so you can see more."
Man: "Mmm yeah – now the fog is gone ... now the sun is there ..."

Obviously there is still a rest of will to see (air) – but otherwise the man wouldn't have asked me for a dream journey to his center at all.

Harry: "Mhm ... can you now better recognize where you are?"
Man: "Yes, on a mountain ... there I stand ... there it goes down to green meadows ... it is also not as high, as I thought ..."
Harry: "Ah yes ..."
Man: "There's something Irish about it, Irish countryside ... yes, a bit 'Lord of the Rings' countryside, but not quite so high ... there's a hill country in front of me ... but nice weather ... the sun is shining ..."

Apparently there is a "beautiful country" below after all. The man also realizes that the mountain he is standing on is not so high and dangerous.

Harry: "Mhm ... You can, if it feels good to you, summon a red ball of wool, tie one end of the red ball of wool around your wrist and then throw it up in the air and tell it to fall down where your center is. ... ... Does that sound good to you?"
Man: "No..."
Harry: "O.K. ... ehm ..."

It sounds like the "golden thread" (German: "red thread") is too direct a method for the man.

Man: "I see a path on the left – there's a path there ... there in the left corner of my eye ... I'm standing on this sand there – that's a path ... and it goes down to the left, I see – but only out of the left corner of my eye ..."

Left is the past – and the man only half sees the way to the "more alive land" below the mountain ...

Harry: "Do you want to go that way?"
Man: "Yeah ... you could do that, right? ... Somehow I can't really get there ... I can see the way, but I can't really move forward ..."
Harry: "Ah! ... You could ask the path if it helps you to go ..."
Man: "It's not quite clear yet, the path ... I only suspect that it goes that way, I only see it out of the corner of my eye ... it's a path ... but I can ask it ... mmm ... if it's a

107

bit clearer ... it's so rigid for me ... I'm looking in the wrong direction to go that way ... so ... I'd just have to turn a bit to the left ..."

Wrong, rigid ... the fear of oneself characterizes the behavior of this man.

Harry: "You could also ask the path if it actually leads to your center."
Man: "Whether the path leads to my center?"
Harry: "Yes ..."
Man: "I don't know how to ask the ..."
Harry: "Just speak to him inwardly ..."
Man: "He doesn't listen to me at all ..."
Harry: "He doesn't listen to you?"
Man: "No."
Harry: "Mhm ..."
Man: "Well, I don't think that's my way ..."

Another evasive maneuver ...

Harry: "O.k. ... how would it feel to just walk straight down the hill?"
Man: "Well, no, that's a jut ... so straight ahead, it does go down a bit ..."
Harry: "Mhm ... and can you go around it somewhere?"
Man: "Well, if I could, I would take this path on the left ... I could imagine that it leads somewhere down there, that goes on the left, but somehow ... uh ... I can't move at all ... so ... I'm relatively static ... well, I can't even turn my head ... so ... so's feeling ... certainly not my body ... so, somehow ... yes, but somehow I can't go straight ahead – there's a ledge – there's a few meters to go, I don't want to go down, I don't want to climb down, it's ... so ... it's a bit too high for me ... I feel a bit trapped right now ..."

Fear ...

Harry: "Yes ... that's how I see it too ... If you like, you can also ask the sun to tell you what you can do best right now."
Man: "I can't see the sun at all – I just see that it's shining ... ehm ... uh ... I can't see it like this ... I don't know if there's a tree in front of it or what ..."

And once again, an evasion ...

Harry: "Yes ... I think something else is needed ... You can put your hand on the ground in front of you, if that feels good to you, and say: 'Here at this point, that

which holds me up here shall now appear.' Because ... you are like trapped there ..."
Man: "Yes ..."
Harry: "And that this should appear now, so that you can see it ..."
Man: "O.k. ..."
Harry: "Can you see something there?"
Man: "I just ... I thought for a moment that I see myself there ... as a child first ... it's all very inconspicuous ... then a picture of today ... then of my nephews ... of my father ... and everything like this ... like a slide show, one after the other, switched through, they change constantly ... it runs like this and again and again there are photos of me ... also very inconspicuous, not quite recognizable ..."
Harry: "You could ask the whole thing to show you the essence of it, the most important thing – because ..."
Man: "Yes, that is already myself ..."
Harry: "Mhm ... How do you look there?"
Man: "I see myself a bit like in the situation now, with my eyes closed ... A mirror of me just sitting here ... lying ... rather gray ... rather a silhouette ... of my reflection ..."

He is afraid of himself ...

Harry: "Can you ask this reflection what it takes to release you?"
Man: "Can I do that ... hm ... it seems to be asleep somehow ... doesn't react at all ..."
Harry: "You could, if you want, try to see what the motive of this reflection is – why it wants to hold you there."
Man: "I could what? The motivation ...?"
Harry: "Yes – the motivation of this reflection ... whether you can see it ... Well, you have called there what holds you there up on this hill ..."
Man: "Yes ..."
Harry: "... and this mirror image must have some reason for doing that."
Man: "It just doesn't react ... the way the reflection is now, nothing can happen ... so ... my impulse ... so ... everything is safe now ... as long as you don't do anything, nothing can go wrong ... It looks, really, like Sleeping Beauty's sleep ... Yes! Exactly! There's something about Sleeping Beauty, so ... that's sleeping there, my reflection and ... yes ... that's ..."

Another evasive maneuver – and an apt self-portrait: Sleeping Beauty.

Harry: "You could also just be really brave and just jump down this slope ..."
Man: "Me?!?"

Harry: "Yes ..."

Man: "But that looks like it's going down deep ..."

Harry: "Yes ... You can also wish that you don't fall down, but float down ..."

Man: "Float? ... I can't float ... ... So, I'm supposed to imagine flying down there now?"

Harry: "Yes ..."

Man: "Mhm ... that's not really my thing ... so now here with the height ... ... no, I can't ... so ... without safety and so ... No! ... Nah, that doesn't feel good ..."

Harry: "Alright ... mmm ... you can try something else if you want ... you can wish for that which gives you security."

Man: "Phew ... now I'm imagining more like a chairlift, where you can strap yourself in ..."

Harry: "Yes?"

Man: "But riding a chairlift isn't really my thing either ..."

Harry: "Okay..."

Man: "Yeah, I've done it before, but ... yeah, I'd do it – already ... before I jump down there like that ... I'd rather take the chairlift ..."

Normally, people on dream trips are thrilled when I suggest they fly ...

Harry: "Wait, maybe something better will come up ... My impression is that this shadowy reflection just wants to hold you up there – so that you don't run off. That's why you could call it in general what gives you courage and security. So, whatever that might be – not only to get down there, but ... Maybe someone who shows you the way, or a lion who gives you strength, or ... whatever ... You can have a look, if you like, if you can call something that gives you this strength and security."

Man: "Pfff ... there comes help from on high ..."

Harry: "What comes from above?"

Man: "Yes, these little helpers that I met during my week in Hamburg (at a meditation weekend) – I'm just becoming aware of them ... that they are standing behind me and that they are carrying me ... this ... yes, this divine part in me ... that can do no wrong ... it's coming right now and supporting me from behind ... mmm ... yes, I just remembered it ... ... So, where should I look again?"

So there is definitely a spiritual aspiration and also a spiritual gift, but at the same time also fear of it ...

Harry: "Just go on downhill ..."

Man: "O.K., then I'll just go ... because actually nothing can happen to me ... I just realized ... Oh yes, there's also a way down!"

Harry: "Which way is that?"
Man: "It goes ... it goes down the hill ... so zigzag ..."
Harry: "To the front?"
Man: "Yes, yes, to the front."
Harry: "Yes, o.k."
Man: "Very rough ... stony ... and you can only see a short stretch ... and there's fog again ... the view is gone again, somehow, but ... you can only see as far as the next corner, where I want to walk down ... but that's even better for me, because then I don't notice the altitude ... Should I just keep walking?"

Fear remains the defining element even now.

Harry: "Yes, I think that's good – just keep walking and see what's coming."
Man: "Yes, I seem to have reached the bottom of the mountain. Phew ... I'm coming now quasi ... the last piece went now through a kind of forest ... there have been now some trees behind me ... and what lies now in front, is foggy again, I cannot really see ..."

The trees are a sign of organized life force.

Harry: "Mhm ... are those helpers still there?"
Man: "Yes, consciously not, but when I now think about it again, yes ... just when I went downstairs I didn't notice them at all, so ... but ... I have the feeling that they are always with me!"
Harry: "Can you ask these helpers to show you ..."
Man: "I don't even know if that's 'the helpers' or if that's one ..."

Another red herring ...

Harry: "It doesn't matter ..."
Man: "It doesn't matter ..."
Harry: "So, the thing that helps you there ... can you ask them to show you where you can find the most important thing for you here?"
Man: "Down here on this mountain, right?"
Harry: "Just there in the landscape where you have arrived now, somewhere there is the most important thing."
Man: "The most important thing for me ... ... uh ... yes ... that ... there's a path, there's a big gate – like a church ... behind this gate there should be ... I should go through it ... I'll just go towards it ... Yes, I'll go into a church ... like the big church in our village used to be – that's how it feels ..."

Obviously religion and spirituality is an important topic for the man – and at the same time he is at war with this topic …

Harry: *"Can you see where the important thing is in this church?"*
Man: *"No, not yet ..."*
Harry: *"Can that, which helps you, lead you there?"*
Man: *"No, difficult – and I'm just wondering what I'm supposed to be doing here ... this is the old church in our village – it's very big ... there's not a church service or anything, there's just the church ... so, to be honest, I'm just a bit confused ... I don't know what I'm supposed to be doing here ..."*
Harry: *"You could, for example, try – because this is a likely spot, if you're looking for the most important thing – to stand behind the altar, where the priest normally stands, and see what happens there ... if something happens there."*
Man: *"O.K. You want me to just go on there?"*
Harry: *"Yes – on this place – not on the altar, but on this place behind the altar."*
Man: *"Eh ... yes ... there are spotlights going on ... so you stand there ... it's like a stage ... Gosh! yes ... there you are already in the center ... yes ..."*

A clear indication that this is the position that is important for the man.

Harry: *"Can your helpers tell you if this is the right position?"*
Man: *"Yes ... definitely! They just nod and grin ..."*
We both laugh ...
Harry: *"Grinning is always good ..."*
Man: *"Well, I have the feeling now that I should ... some message ... I have the feeling that I'm really in front of an audience ... but I don't even know what to say ... so ... I just think so, um ..."*

A first hint at the cause of the fear: the feeling of having to perform something, having to be something specific, having to do something specific … This looks like excessive conformity that has led to a loss of self.

Harry: *"Just ask your helpers if there's anything you can do there right now that makes sense."*
Man: *"I have a feeling they're saying, 'It doesn't matter what you do – you just have to be there.'"*

One can hardly formulate the remedy for this man more clearly …

Harry: *"All right – then just stay there and see how it feels."*

Man: "Pff ... yes, it feels quite good, but I have the feeling that I'm doing somersaults in my head and flying around in the area ... like in such a merry-go-round, but very positive, so ... so somehow, so half weightless, but it's all in my head... as if I'm doing somersaults in my head ... and floating around ... but no clear picture somehow ... so ... so I just have to be ... just be there somehow ... as if I don't have any task at all ... as if I'm just acting as a transmitter ... that's what's happening right now ... as if I can pass on something ... maybe something ... something ... maybe as a messenger ... it just seems to me ..."

The somersaults are the repressed antithesis to the rigidity and immobility and fear ... the real essence of the man will be somewhere in between these two extremes.

The somersaults take place in the head – so it is about the Third Eye, i.e. that the man looks too much after what the others expect him to do ...

Harry: "Ask your helpers if you are there to be an ambassador."
Man: "They're grinning like that again ... I get the feeling they don't take me seriously at all ... pfff ... yeah, seems so ..."
Harry: "Would it feel good for you, these helpers or the helper, that they appear in front of you? That you could have a good look at them?"
Man: "I don't think they're so ... that they have such a figure."
Harry: "You could just ask them and see what happens..."
Man: "That they show themselves to me?"
Harry: "Yes – why not?"
Man: "Now comes a picture of my mother ... ... of 'a friend – that was there before ... who also works spiritually ... then another friend ... so, these are already familiar faces ... (laughs) ... my wife's sister is also there ... Yes, these are all people who have influenced me ... positively influenced me – up to the point today, yes ..."

Again a red herring – the man fears the perception of his own soul like the devil fears holy water ... if he would see exactly who he is, he would not be able to adapt – and that would be a problem, because he would then be confronted with his fears ...

Here it is important to proceed gently – persistently, but gently ...

Harry: "You could also try something else: You could simply call your own center, whether it can appear to you ... yes ... as a shape. So yours or your soul or ... whatever you call it ..."
Man: "As a shape?"
Harry: "Yes – that you can see it before you. So you get to know what it looks like."
Man: "Pfff ... ... there's nothing ... there's something more like ... no, there's ... that's not proper ... like ..."

113

That are just some euphemisms for "fear."

Harry: "It's all right ..."
Man: "Or maybe there's 'resistance' – I don't know about that ... kind of ..."
Harry: "That's not proper? Does that refer to the fact that this has a shape or that ..."
Man: "No, to ... question that at all ... somehow I'm also a little afraid that maybe nothing will come ... that there's nothing ... that maybe I don't have a real soul or something ..."
Harry: "Oh, I see – the subject as such scares you a bit ..."
Man: "Yes ... that maybe it's all just gibberish ... and there we are again with the 'dancers in the dark' (a song he has composed) ... What do we know? ... Yes, now comes quite a questioning of the whole, of what I have just built up there with the helpers and the stage ... somehow I just think: 'If all this is not true at all ... would not be there ... and everything is just ... a brainwave' ..."

Now the fog is in his head and confuses him and prevents him from drawing logical conclusions and then acting on the basis of these insights.

Harry: "At the moment you just look at what's coming – you don't have to ask if it's true or not ..."
Man: "I'm slipping into the mind, nah?"
Harry: "Yes ... You can just look at the images that come up. You can think about it later."
Man: "Mhm ..."
Harry: "It started when you said ... What was that? ... Whether I'm allowed to do that or something like that? ... Whether my center will come, whether it has a shape – maybe there won't be any ..."
Man: "Yes, whether I'm entitled to do that, whether I'm allowed to do that ... you don't do that ... or so ... to question that at all ... to ask a question there ..."

The man, because of his fears, twists what he actually intends to do on this dream journey. It is typical for some types of fear that they block everything far in advance to the actual fear topic, so that one cannot even get close to the fear topic. This is a form of self-protection ...

Harry: "You're not actually questioning it – you want to get to know it ..."
Man: "Actually, I guess, yes, I'd like to get to know it."
Harry: "In that respect ... you can actually just speak it out ... that your soul, your

114

center just appears to you, so that you know what it looks like."

Man: "Yes, then it should really show itself now, so, I would like to get to know it ... I also thought I had already spoken with it once at a family constellation ... there was such a bright light ... but a figure ... that is very hesitant, so ... as if my soul was afraid of me ... afraid to show itself to me ..."

Harry: "You see a bright light?"

Man: "Yes – a kind of harbinger somehow ... only I ..."

Harry: "What do you think about going into that bright light?"

Man: "No ... that's a little bit below me ... so, when I look down, so ... that goes towards the ground somehow ... that's ... ... I can go in there ... ... now it's like at the beginning again – now I'm standing at such a point, it's all foggy ..."

Another evasion attempt …

Harry: "Is that fog or is that light?"

Man: "Yes, light, but somehow ... somehow ... at least I don't see anything other than ..."

Harry: "You can ask the light if it is your center."

Man: "No ... no, no ..."

Here the fear of being true to oneself becomes obvious – because that is exactly where the recognition of one's own soul leads.

Harry: "Are you saying 'no' ... you're not asking that now, or is the light saying it's not your center?"

Man: "No ... I don't know myself ... I have the feeling that I'm not seen here at all, so ... but the light is also not ... I can't grasp it ... it's more like ... it's space somehow ... I don't know ... ... A room with a blue ceiling, in which I'm now ... but there's also nothing else, somehow ..."

Harry: "Can you touch the blue ceiling?"

Man: "No ... no, not anymore ... now it's all dissolving again, somehow ... such a change ... like such a sky ..."

He quickly runs away … here the center might become visible …

Harry: "You could try something completely different: You could tell your center that when it feels like doing something, to show you something, to tell you something, to do something – whatever – that it should just do it and you see what happens. ... Does that sound good to you?"

Man: "I can ask that, but from my feeling ... from my feeling I have the feeling that

115

my center doesn't want to communicate with me ... I don't know why – but there's somehow nothing ... well, I'm somehow ignored a bit, so ... I just thought that again ... that then somehow fizzles out like that ..."

This is a reversal of the facts: The soul has nothing against talking to the man, but the man is afraid to see his center – and to be faithful to it (and consequently to himself).

Harry: "Then you could ask why your center ignores you, and if you see it correctly."
Man: "Yes, seems ... seems to be a bit offended ..."
Harry: "For what reason?"
Man: "Yes, because I haven't noticed her for a long time, right? I didn't pay attention to them, I didn't ... uh ... I didn't ... I didn't take their wishes seriously ... I've already had that in a family constellation ... I just remembered that ..."
Harry: "Would you like to do it differently?"
Man: "Do what differently?"
Harry: "Just perceive your soul and get what it wants, and then see if you want to do that."
Man: "Yes, of course, in principle, but I am very skeptical ... I can understand my soul ... I am always very cautious and always like to take the easy way ... and, ... well ... these are a bit empty words, when I say this to the soul ... I don't know ... it seems to have a little bit of inauthenticity, but ... and it is now a bit offended and ignores me, exactly! ... This is now based on mutuality, it seems ... this now seems to be a bit of a stalemate situation ... I just feel a bit stupid ..."

The image that others want something from him is very strong in the man – and that the others are offended when they don't get what they want from him.

For me this dream journey meanwhile is a bid like a long game of chess against the fears of this man …

Harry: "Well, you could tell her, for example – well, if that's true for you – that you have the feeling that the situation is actually a bit stupid, that you would like to change that and that you don't know exactly how – and that you would like to explore together with her how you can have a different relationship to each other. ... So, if that's true, you could tell her that."
Man: "Yes ... pfff ... yes, that's already very emotional ... because I just don't know what to do, I don't want to make any false promises, so ... I've already talked to my soul about it, then ... somehow I keep forgetting her and keep leaving her at the side and ... I somehow can't do anything else – I've got my everyday life and my problems

116

and all the shit that you put in front of you, that ..."

Here the problem becomes very clear – he is always looking at the judgment of others and their supposed demands on him.

Harry: "You don't have to promise her anything ..."
Man: "O.k. ..."
Harry: "You can just tell her: 'Listen, I realize that this is not optimal yet, I would like to improve it, I have no idea if I can do it or what I actually have to do, but if you think this is good too, then let's just try it out."
Man: "Yes, how is that supposed to work, if I always resist it, when the soul has an idea and then I immediately flatten it ... then that's ... then it will end up back where it is now ..."
Harry: "Yes – that's right. But it's also true that some corner of you isn't quite happy with this state of affairs – otherwise you probably wouldn't be here at all."
Man: "Yes ..."
Harry: "And you can at least tell your soul that you see that it's not good like that, and that you don't have any idea yet how you can change it ... You can at least tell it that you realize that it's not good like that yet."
Man: "Yes, that's right ... that's all I can do ..."
Harry: "Nope ... more is not useful then ... but you can just tell her that and see how she reacts."
Man: "... ... ... yes, that's o.k. in any case ... yes, that feels very stimulating ... that takes away my feeling of guilt a bit ..." (He cries a little ...)

Now he has expressed the problem himself: He feels guilty when he doesn't do what the others want – including fulfilling the supposed wishes of his own soul.

Harry: "That's nice ... ... If that suits you, you can also ask your soul if it wants to tell you something."
Man: "No, there's not really anything coming ... it's more of a peace situation, but I don't get any real information ... but that doesn't really seem to be necessary right now ... it's more like a 'going on' ..."
Harry: "Well, that's good. ... My feeling is that this is enough for now. ... How is it with you?"
Man: "Yes ..."
Harry: "Then you can see if there's anything you want to say to your helpers or to your soul, or say goodbye or thank you or whatever – and then you can go to the entrance symbol and return through the symbol again."
Man: "All I can say is I can keep my eyes open, but I can't promise anything ..."

Harry: "You're not supposed to promise anything ... You can just say 'Nice to have seen you!'"
Man: "O.k."

In the end, the man has found the courage and the realization that he doesn't have to do anything for his soul ...

V 25.   Situations

Situations are also images that can be understood with the help of the "language of the moon". There are two forms of situation-images:

   - One form is the omen. Here something small and conspicuous happens, which stands in analogy to something large. The conspicuousness is necessary, so that one notices the small event at all.
   For example, one may see another person stumble three times in a row. In such a situation, it would be obvious to see if there is something that one could stumble over oneself – and then be cautious about this issue.
   One can also explain omens astrologically: The current planetary position "influences" all things in the same way, which is why all things behave similarly. Therefore, what you see in others could also be significant for you.

   - The second form is also a striking event – but an event that repeats itself in the life of the person concerned and is therefore one of his "patterns".
   If one finally allows oneself a vacation after 20 years of constant work and no vacation, and then this vacation cannot be taken because of the Corona virus, it is obvious to ask oneself what in the person concerned so systematically prevents the enjoyment of life …

V 26. Imaginations

Imagination is the counterpart to the understanding of images: the creation of images – for which you, of course, need an understanding of the nature of images. Imagination is a very essential element in magic and partly also in meditation, because with the help of will and imagination one can direct the life force and thus also events.

It is important to know and respect the rules of the "language of the moon", so that the imagined images lead to what you want to achieve.

The most important rule is that everything should be imagined in the simplest possible pictorial way. This means, for example, that one should always imagine the desired state and not the obstacle – this is the so-called "positive thinking".

The importance of the images one imagines or concentrates on can be checked by the smilie attempt:

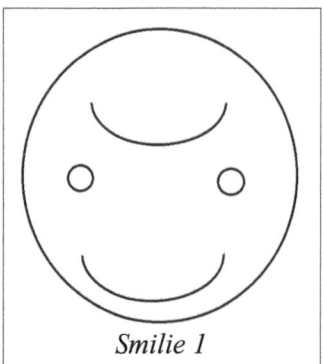

Smilie 1

For the "smilie experiment" one needs a sheet of papier on which the "smilie" shown on the left is drawn. This sheet with the drawing is placed at the edge of a table in such a way that a person standing in front of the table sees this picture as shown on the left.

Now person A stands in front of the table and spreads his arms to the left and right like a "T" and like a cross, respectively. A should keep his arms in this posture as much as possible during the following trials and not change them.

Person B stands behind A and places his right hand on A's right elbow and his left hand on A's left elbow.

A looks at the smilie and B presses on A's elbows. Nothing happens – B can lean on A's elbows and let his feet dangle in the air.

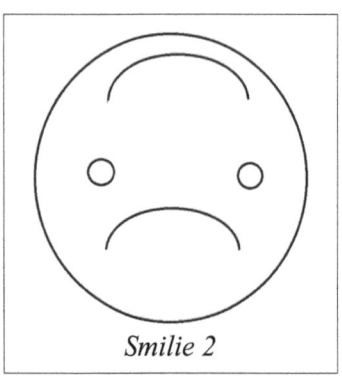

Smilie 2

Now the smilie is turned over (see the illustration on the left) and the experiment is repeated in the same way - and A's arms fold down powerlessly. A is unable to keep his arms extended at the top.

What happened here? Obviously, looking at the picture has a greater effect on A than A's conscious decision to keep his arms up.

Two modes of action are possible: on the one hand, the "depressed smilie" could suggest to A that he is now failing in his attempt to keep his arms up. On the other hand, the two "Ω" of the mouth and the forehead crease of the smilie A could suggest that he should drop his arms, so that they then have the same posture together with his shoulders as the "Ω".

This experiment shows that the subconscious also reacts to external information and not only to the decision in the waking consciousness. Obviously, the impression that the sight of the "Ω" makes on the subconscious is significantly greater than the decision to keep the arms up.

Concentration on the "Ω"-smilie by the waking consciousness in the "office" (A looks at the smilie during the experiment) apparently sends an "office messenger" with the message into the "archive" of the subconsciousness that the "Ω"-state is to be reached – then the subconsciousness sends this message to the muscles of the arms.

This attempt shows clearly what suggestions, advertisements, demagogy and the like can be capable of when one no longer consciously controls what one's waking consciousness concentrates on.

(More details may be found in my book „Auto-Movement for Beginners".)

V 27. Agreements with the subconscious mind

The agreements with the subconsciousness use the normal language, which shows that the ususal "Mercury language" (words) can be translated, at least partially, by the subconsciousness into the "lunar language" (images).

The situations in which this language is used, however, is the realm of image-language.

V 27. a) Lantern posts

As a teenager and as a young adult I often had trouble with myself and inwardly berated myself. At some point I noticed that every time I ran into a lamppost or a tree and then lay on the ground with my head hurting (which often happened to me at that time), I had once again inwardly berated myself directly beforehand.

Thereupon I asked my subconsciousness that I instead only lightly bump against something with my right hand. In return, I committed myself to pause immediately when I bumped into anything with my right hand, and then look at what I had just thought and felt. I asked my subconsciousness that if I ever failed to notice, it would only slowly increase the cues.

Since then, I have almost never bumped my head.

V 28. Agreements with the Gods

One can use the lunar language also in conversations with the gods – if one wants, one can also speak of "collective subconsciousness" instead of "gods". This also makes clear that the gods speak the same language as the subconsciousness, because the collective subconsciousness is the telepathic-telekinetic interconnection of the individual consciousnesses of the single human beings.

V 28. a) Money

I experienced the clearest example of such an arrangement after I became self-employed as a consultant and writer.

Even as a child, I always had the image in my mind of starving and freezing to death under a railroad bridge. That's why I kept looking for security and support – which no longer exists as a self-employed person … there's no one standing protectively between you and the world.

I made it clear to myself again and again that one cannot starve so easy in Germany, but that was of little use – it reached my mind, but not my inner world of images.

One day I simply realized that I needed support, that there was simply no other way. I don't know why, but I suddenly turned to "those up there" (soul, gods, etc.) and told them that I now trust them. Just like that. Without reasoning. Without consideration. I simply decided it.

Since then I don't have this fear anymore and I have always had enough money. When I was short of money, I told them up there that they had to send me money if they liked the way I was living – which they did every time.

English Books by Harry Eilenstein

- Living Magic (261 p.)
- The Synthesis of Physics and Magic (192 p.)
- Telepathy for Beginners (60 p.)
- Telepathy for Advanced Learners (52 p.)
- Telekinesis for Beginners (56 p.)
- Life Force for Beginners (76 p.)
- Astral Projection for Beginners (60 p.)
- Meditation for Beginners (60 p.)
- Prophecy for Beginners (60 p.)
- Ritual Magic for Beginners (64 p.)
- Magic Chant for Beginners (108 p.)
- Invocations for Beginners (52 p.)
- Evocations for Beginners (62 p.)
- Auto-Movement for Beginners (60 p.)
- Elves for Beginners (56 p.)
- Hypnosis for Beginners (56 p.)
- Love Magic for Beginners (52 p.)
- Money Magic for Beginners (60 p.)
- Magic Objects for Beginners (64 p.)

- Shamanism for Beginners (52 p.)
- Language of the Moon – for Beginners (128 p.)
- Self Knowledge for Beginners (60 p.)
- Astrology for Beginners (112 p.)
- Number Symbolism for Beginners (64 p.)
- Mandalas for Beginners (76 p.)
- Crop Circles for Beginners (344 p.)
- Feng Shui for Beginners (96 p.)

These books will be puplished soon:

- Kundalini for Beginners
- Chakra-Magic for Beginners
- Magic Research for Beginners
- Symbolism of Numbers for Beginners
- Da'ath-Magic for Beginners
- Magic for Beginners – Anthology I
- Magic for Beginners – Anthology II
- Magic for Beginners – Anthology III
- Magic for Beginners – Anthology IV

Bücher von Harry Eilenstein

Religion allgemein
- Die sieben Schritte des Lebens (428 S.)
- Muttergöttin und Schamanen (168 S.)
- Göbekli Tepe (472 S.)
- Die Göttin von Göbekli Tepe (144 S.)
- Die Biographie des Teufels (144 S.)
- Totempfähle (440 S.)
- Christus (60 S.)
- Dakini (80 S.)
- Vajra (76 S.)

Ägypten
- Hathor und Re 1: Götter und Mythen im Alten Ägypten (432 S.)
- Hathor und Re 2: Die altägyptische Religion – Ursprünge, Kult und Magie (396 S.)
- Isis (508 S.)

Indogermanen
- Die Entwicklung der indogermanischen Religionen (700 S.)
- Wurzeln und Zweige der indogermanischen Religion (224 S.)

Germanen
- Die Götter der Germanen (87 Bände – siehe nächste Seite)
- Odin (300 S.)

Kelten
- Cernunnos (690 S.)
- Taliesin (228 S.)
- Der Kessel von Gundestrup (220 S.)
- Der Chiemsee-Kessel (76)

Psychologie
- Über die Freude (100 S.)
- Das Geheimnis des inneren Friedens (252 S.)
- Das Beziehungsmandala (52 S.)
- Gefühle und ihre Verwandlungen (404 S.)
- einsgerichtet (140 S.)
- Liebe und Eigenständigkeit (216 S.)
- Von innerer Fülle zu äußerem Gedeihen (52 S.)

Heilung
- Die Symbolik der Krankheiten (76 S.)

Kunst
- Herz des Tanzes – Tanz des Herzens (160 S.)

Drama
- König Athelstan (104 S.)

Bücher von Harry Eilenstein

„Magie für Anfänger"	Magie

- Telepathie für Anfänger (60 S.)
- Telepathie für Fortgeschrittene (52 S.)
- Telekinese für Anfänger (52 S.)
- Lebenskraft für Anfänger (60 S.)
- Meditation für Anfänger (56 S.)
- Kundalini für Anfänger (100 S.)
- Hypnose für Anfänger (56 S.)
- Auto-Movement für Anfänger (56 S.)
- Chakra-Magie für Anfänger (148 S.)
- Astralreisen für Anfänger (56 S.)
- Astrologie für Anfänger (120 S.)
- Ritual-Magie für Anfänger (56 S.)
- Mandalas für Anfänger (68 S.)
- Geldzauber für Anfänger (56 S.)
- Liebeszauber für Anfänger (52 S.)
- Invokationen für Anfänger (52 S.)
- Evokationen für Anfänger (60 S.)
- Elfen für Anfänger (56 S.)
- Magie-Forschung für Anfänger (140 S.)
- Selbsterkenntnis für Anfänger (52 S.)
- Zahlensymbolik für Anfänger (60 S.)
- Die Sprache des Mondes – für Anfänger (116 S.)
- Zaubergesänge für Anfänger (100 S.)
- Zukunftschau für Anfänger (60 S.)
- Schamanismus für Anfänger (52 S.)
- Magische Gegenstände für Anfänger (68 S.)
- Da'ath-Magie für Anfänger (64 S.)
- Kornkreise für Anfänger (348 S.)
- Feng Shui für Anfänger (96 S.)
- Magie für Anfänger – Sammelband I (696 S.)
- Magie für Anfänger – Sammelband II (664 S.)
- Magie für Anfänger – Sammelband III (580 S.)
 	
„Traumreisen"
- Traumreisen zu Heilpflanzen (700 S.)
	- Handbuch für Zauberlehrlinge (408 S.)
	- Tarot (104 S.)
	- Physik und Magie (184 S.)
	- Die Synthese von Physik und Magie (200S.)
	- Die Magie-Formel (156 S.)
	- Krafttiere – Tiergöttinnen – Tiertänze (112 S.)
	- Schwitzhütten (524 S.)
	- Mythen und Magie der Harfe (116 S.)
	- Magie heute – Berichte aus der Praxis (288 S.)
	
	Meditation
	- Der Lebenskraftkörper (230 S.)
	- Die Chakren (100 S.)
	- Das Chakren-System mit den Nebenchakren (296 S.)
	- Organe und Chakren (64 S.)
	- Die platonischen Körper in den Chakren (156 S.)
	- Meditation (140 S.)
	- Drachenfeuer (124 S.)
	- Kundalini I (676 S.)
	- Reinkarnation (156 S.)
	- einsgerichtet (140 S.)
	
	Astrologie
	- Astrologie (496 S.)
	- Photo-Astrologie (428 S.)
	- Die astrologischen Aspekte (88 S.)
	- Horoskop und Seele (120 S.)
	
	Kabbala
	- Kursus der praktischen Kabbala (150 S.)
	- Eltern der Erde (450 S.)
	- Blüten des Lebensbaumes:
	  - Die Struktur des kabbalistischen Lebensbaumes (370 S.)
	  - Der kabbalistische Lebensbaum als Forschungshilfsmittel (580 S.)
	  - Der kabbalistische Lebensbaum als spirituelle Landkarte (520 S.)

Die Themen der 87 Bände der Reihe „Die Götter der Germanen"

1. Die Entwicklung der germanischen Religion
2. Lexikon der germanischen Religion
3. Der ursprüngliche Göttervater Tyr
4. Tyr in der Unterwelt: der Schmied Wieland
5. Tyr in der Unterwelt: der Riesenkönig   Teil 1
6. Tyr in der Unterwelt: der Riesenkönig   Teil 2
7. Tyr in der Unterwelt: der Zwergenkönig
8. Der Himmelswächter Heimdall
9. Der Sommergott Baldur
10. Der Meeresgott: Ägir, Hler und Njörd
11. Der Eibengott Ullr
12. Die Zwillingsgötter Alcis
13. Der neue Göttervater Odin   Teil 1
14. Der neue Göttervater Odin   Teil 2
15. Der Fruchtbarkeitsgott Freyr
16. Der Chaos-Gott Loki
17. Der Donnergott Thor
18. Der Priestergott Hönir
19. Die Göttersöhne
20. Die unbekannteren Götter
21. Die Göttermutter Frigg
22. Die Liebesgöttin: Freya und Menglöd
23. Die Erdgöttinnen
24. Die Korngöttin Sif
25. Die Apfel-Göttin Idun
26. Die Hügelgrab-Jenseitsgöttin Hel
27. Die Meeres-Jenseitsgöttin Ran
28. Die unbekannteren Jenseitsgöttinnen
29. Die unbekannteren Göttinnen
30. Die Nornen
31. Die Walküren
32. Die Zwerge
33. Der Urriese Ymir
34. Die Riesen
35. Die Riesinnen
36. Mythologische Wesen
37. Mythologische Priester und Priesterinnen
38. Sigurd/Siegfried
39. Helden und Göttersöhne
40. Die Symbolik der Vögel und Insekten
41. Die Symbolik der Schlangen, Drachen und Ungeheuer
42.a Die Symbolik der Herdentiere I
42.b Die Symbolik der Herdentiere II
43. Die Symbolik der Raubtiere
44. Die Symbolik der Wassertiere und sonstigen Tiere
45. Die Symbolik der Pflanzen
46. Die Symbolik der Farben
47. Die Symbolik der Zahlen
48. Die Symbolik von Sonne, Mond und Sternen
49.a Das Jenseits I – Das Hügelgrab
49.b Das Jenseits II – Der Jenseitsweg
50. Seelenvogel, Utiseta und Einweihung
51. Wiederzeugung und Wiedergeburt
52. Elemente der Kosmologie
53. Der Weltenbaum
54. Die Symbolik der Himmelsrichtungen und der Jahreszeiten
55.a Mythologische Motive I
55.b Mythologische Motive II
56. Der Tempel
57. Die Einrichtung des Tempels
58. Priesterin – Seherin – Zauberin – Hexe
59. Priester – Seher – Zauberer
60. Rituelle Kleidung und Schmuck
61. Skalden und Skaldinnen
62. Kriegerinnen und Ekstase-Krieger
63. Die Symbolik der Körperteile
64.a Magie und Ritual I
64.b Magie und Ritual II
64.c Magie und Ritual III
65. Gestaltwandlungen
66.a Magische Angriffs-Waffen
66.b Magische Verteidigungs-Waffen
67. Magische Werkzeuge und Gegenstände
68. Zaubersprüche
69. Göttermet
70. Zaubertränke
71. Träume, Omen und Orakel
72. Runen
73. Sozial-religiöse Rituale
74. Weisheiten und Sprichworte
75. Kenningar
76. Rätsel
77. Die vollständige Edda des Snorri Sturluson
78. Frühe Skaldenlieder
79.a Mythologische Sagas I
79.b Mythologische Sagas II
80. Hymnen an die germanischen Götter